Small City
in a
Big Valley

Small City
in a
Big Valley

THE STORY
OF DUNCAN

Tom Henry

HARBOUR PUBLISHING

Published by

HARBOUR PUBLISHING
P.O. Box 219
Madeira Park, BC Canada
V0N 2H0

Cover, page design and composition by Martin Nichols, Lionheart Graphics
Edited by Lorna Jackson
Printed and bound in Canada

Photo credits: BCARS=British Columbia Archives & Records Service; CVM=Cowichan Valley Museum; QMS=Queen Margaret's School

Harbour Publishing acknowledges the financial support of the Government of Canada through the Book Publishing Industry Development Program (BPIDP) and the Canada Council for the Arts, and the Province of British Columbia through the British Columbia Arts Council, for its publishing activities.

THE CANADA COUNCIL | LE CONSEIL DES ARTS
FOR THE ARTS | DU CANADA
SINCE 1957 | DEPUIS 1957

Canadian Cataloguing in Publication Data

Henry, Tom, 1961–
    Small city in a big valley

Includes index
ISBN 1-55017-212-3

    1. Duncan (B.C.)—History. I. Title.
FC3849.D85H46 1999   971.1'2   C99-910894-8
F1089.5.D8H46 1999

Contents

Introduction

MUCH OF THE RESEARCH for *Small City in a Big Valley* was done the summer of 1998 in the archives of the Cowichan Historical Society in Duncan, BC. The archives occupy the second floor of the train station, a long CPR-red building in the city's core. The second floor used to be the station master's residence. Archival records are kept in the former bedroom and researchers work at a paddock-sized table in the living room. My spot was at the table's south end. To check the time all I had to do was glance up at the city hall clock. To note details on a Station Street historical building, I looked out the window.

In the afternoon, in the summer, the archives got very hot. Portable fans blew muggy air from one part of the room to another part of the room. When the heat got to be too much, I'd cross Canada Avenue to a deli and buy a soft drink. Then I'd flop into the shade of one of the red oaks in the cenotaph park, sip cool cola and think back to a time—before Duncan was thick with traffic and franchise eateries; before its dusty streets echoed with the sound of horses' hooves and wagon wheels; before, even, it was fields and orchards—to a spring day in 1864, when a slender young man came striding through dense timber no more than a block from where I was reclining.

William Chalmers Duncan was twenty-eight years old. Work-leaned, narrow-faced, he had a thatched beard and a head of tufted brown hair that never stayed completely flat. He was an expert axeman and had, it was said, a gift with animals (his honeybees always swarmed for Good Friday). William Duncan was raised in Sarnia, Ontario, one of thirteen children born to a Scots-descended family. He had left home for the west coast and the Fraser River goldfields. Like thousands of other fortune seekers, however, he discovered in

Victoria that the so-called gold rush was anything but: every available ship, scow and dugout had been commandeered for the Strait of Georgia crossing. He eventually got as far as the Fraser Valley; then, fearing his provisions would run low before spring thaw, wisely retreated to the capital. It was there that William Duncan heard of a government scheme to open a rich island valley for settlement.

After Victoria and New Westminster, the Cowichan Valley was the new frontier of the 1860s. The area's potential for farm and settlement had been recognized twenty years earlier, by James Douglas, but at that time it was under control of the Hudson's Bay Company, which was more interested in keeping the west coast a fur preserve than in opening it to settlement. The HBC's plan faltered when gold was discovered in 1858. An influx of American miners into the unsettled territory threatened to give the expansion-minded United States government reason to annex the entire west coast. The HBC lease expired, a colonial government was established and overnight, settlement became a priority. Land prices were lowered 80 percent and a pre-emption plan, whereby ownership of land was contingent on a steady transformation from forest to farm, was set up to encourage energetic young men to take up land.

In 1862, seventy-eight prospective settlers, including William Duncan, shipped into Cowichan Bay on the Royal Navy vessel *Hecate*. Many settlers went inland but William Duncan stayed near the bay. The land wasn't to his liking—why, I have no idea—but in 1863 he went to the Cariboo goldfields and found wage work hewing mine props and bridge stringers. By the time he returned, much of the south valley was claimed. Acting on a tip from a settler, Duncan took a canoe up the Cowichan River. At the Indian village of Somena he disembarked and walked northward. The bush was rampant and difficult to traverse, the timber so thick it formed a canopy overhead. At the top of a knoll,

William Chalmers Duncan
(1836–1919), in 1883.
CVM 998.07.1.6

William Duncan paused by a densely branched western red cedar. The tree grew at what would later be the corner of Trunk Road and Brae Road in downtown Duncan.

Slipping off his canvas rucksack, William Duncan scaled the cedar, he later recalled, stepping up the spiralling branches as if on a stairway. He stopped only when high enough to see over the tassels of the surrounding timber. The view encompassed thousands of hectares. To the west and north, the green sweep of timbered mountains disappeared up the U-shaped valley. To the south, the winding course of the Cowichan River was marked by a corridor of cottonwoods and to the east was the shimmer of Cowichan Bay, some 5 kilometres distant.

For William Duncan, though, the dominant feature was the immediately encircling bottomland. Clad in the variegated greens of alder, maple and cedar, it swept away from his treetop perch on all sides, an undulating rug of foliage on rich river-washed soil. The land would require a huge amount of work before it could be deemed settled. Peering from between the limbs of the cedar, the twenty-eight-year-old Duncan could read into the untouched countryside a future visage of fields and ponds, of fences and cows and snorting pigs, of a log cabin with a cobblestone chimney and a ropey twist of woodsmoke. It was the kind of vision on which to build a city.

Small City in a Big Valley is a true story. It begins with a man in a tree, ends with a man on a totem pole and includes some of the major and many of the not-so-major themes in Duncan's history: Native use of the land; settler architecture and urban development; gentlemen immigrants; World War I; Norah Denny and Queen Margaret's School; Sue Lem Bing's Chinatown; internment of the Japanese; Mayor Wragg's highway blockade and the ongoing post-1960s reinvention of the city's self-image.

The story is based on archival sources but is informed by my own experiences. This point I want to make clear. I am fond of Duncan. I was born there. I attended Duncan Elementary, Cowichan Senior Secondary. I played road hockey in front of Wayne Jackson's home in Centennial Heights, thumbed magazines at Chow Bros. Grocery, sipped cold Tzouhalem Hotel beer under the steely eye of Cece-the-Bartender. Some Duncan backyards may still have ricks of fir and alder I sold when I was a woodcutter. I think Duncan is a fine place. I return often to visit my family.

My mother is from a well-connected English clan; my father is a transplanted Ontario farmer. They managed the Silver Bridge Inn and later ran a local battery shop. The stories my mother told around the kitchen table of our Castle Street home were generally positive and concerned character-building teachers of her youth who prohibited coughing, or they were about the Evans, Whittome or Stone families (the latter at one time a prominent lumbering clan, some of whom are my cousins). My father's take on Duncan was somewhat different. He would come home from the hotel smelling of sweet drinks, grumbling about the kleptomaniacal matron of a founding family who had a taste for hotel silverware, or jerks who drained the swimming pool, or the times BC Premier W.A.C. Bennett used to whistle up from Victoria for a ministerial tête-à-tête at the Silver Bridge Inn and insisted on using the ladies' washroom. The accounts were so divergent I grew up thinking Duncan was not one town but many.

Nothing I've learned since has changed that impression. There are lots of stories about Duncan. Some of the good ones are in this book.

"We Did Not Resist You"

WILLIAM DUNCAN'S ANCESTORS were still roaming the Scottish Highlands in bare feet and animal skins when another pioneer first glimpsed the Cowichan Valley. Nothing is known about this individual, except that he or she was of a band of hunter-gatherers who colonized land emerging from the glacial retreat, some four to seven thousand years ago. Clad in furs, adept in fishing and wood-work, they were descendants of the ancient migrants who crossed the north-ern land bridge linking Asia with North America, then slowly made their way south into coastal valleys.

These early wanderers were the forebears of the Cowichan Valley's Native peoples. The Cowichans were members of the Coast Salish, a nation whose territory included the southeast coast of Vancouver Island and the Lower

Several weirs spanned the Cowichan River at the Native village of Somena. Large-scale weir fishing for salmon contin-ued on the river until the 1930s. BCARS H-06525

Mainland. Favoured with the region's generous climate and abundant food, the Cowichans developed a complex, expressive culture. The foundation of the culture was a webbing network of family relations, or kin groups, each with its own longhouses, stories, ceremonies and uniquely carved totem poles. Each kin group controlled economic resources, such as a berry patch, a fishing station, a hunting ground. When a number of kin groups shared the same locality they formed tribes.

The Cowichans comprised seven tribes, each represented by a village: Malahat, Kilpahlas and Khenipsen were oceanfront settlements; Koksilah was on the Koksilah River; Clemclemaluts and Comiaken were on the tidewater reaches of the Cowichan estuary; Quamichan and Somena were a short distance east and south, respectively, of the current city of Duncan on the banks of the Cowichan River. Quamichan and Somena people were essentially riverine. They harvested salmon from weirs that spanned the river, they travelled the river in dugouts carved from cedars that grew along its banks. They named

The Great Flood

Though the Duncan area was incidental to daily Cowichan Native life, it was physically central to several of their more important legends, including the story of the Great Flood. According to one version of the legend, the valley was once deluged with an endless rain. Low-lying land soon disappeared under rising waters and the people of the valley sought refuge on Mt. Tzouhalem. Then unnamed, the mountain was smaller than S'wukus (Mt. Prevost) or the surrounding hills but it miraculously sheltered the Cowichans from the valley bottom. No matter how high the water rose, the top of the mountain was always above the surface. Eventually Peep-ahm—"the rising mountain-top rock"—was the only dry land north of Sooke. Everything else was submerged. When the waters receded, the survivors found a giant frog warming himself on the side of the mountain. In Hul'qumi'num, the language of the Cowichan people, the word for basking in the sun is *s'khowtzun*. The survivors decided to take this name for themselves. *S'khowtzun* became *Khowtzun* and *Khowtzun* became Cowichan. Both the mountain and the people of the valley were called Cowichans.

Khowtzun Mountain was later given the name of a powerful and deranged Cowichan warrior. The boy-killing Tzuhalem terrorized his fellow tribesmen until a Kuper Island medicine woman cut him up with a knife and spread the body parts over nearby beaches. The name of the mountain has changed but the image of the frog remains.

many places on the river, and the names are as descriptive as they are beautiful. For instance, *su'weemqun*, "water makes a quiet sound"; *hwehwi'qus*, "rubbing; just missing each other"; *shtsmunuyul*, "place to get dolls." On the east side of the present White Bridge, the Cowichan River intersects a coho- and trout-bearing creek that was called *hwusa'um*, meaning "cold." The stream is cold, it is said, because a mother and father once punished a son who would not share a fish by placing him in a coffin and submerging the coffin in the stream. The boy drowned. As his body cooled, so did the water in the creek and the air above it.

Reeds picked from local lakes were woven into baskets, hats and mats. BCARS D-08941

Inland from Somena is a distinctive rise known by villagers as both the Mound and Strawberry Hill. To the north of Strawberry Hill, where city hall rises, was a nameless fluvial plain rich in vegetation and lauded as good deer range. Beyond that was a rise of heavy timber, also nameless, where the Somena people went for quiet and contemplation. It is now called Hospital Hill.

From the clustered longhouses at Somena, villagers walked past Strawberry Hill to the reed-picking grounds at Somenos Lake. From here, the Somena people could see the distinctive twin outcroppings of a mountain they called S'wukus, marked on current maps as Mt. Prevost. According to legend, two brothers and a unicorn-like dog once dropped from the sky onto the slopes of S'wukus. Syalutsa and Stutsun were genesis beings akin to the biblical Adam. Syalutsa, whose dog the mountain was named for, was said to have begotten the Cowichans; his brother Stutsun was said to have begotten the Chemainus tribes. The two groups were geographically distinct but for a small encampment on the north bank of the Cowichan River, a few metres east of where the Trans-Canada Highway now crosses into Duncan. Siyaykw, or Xelaltxw ("painted house"), was once a settlement of seven longhouses. Stutsun, it was said, founded this village before going north and his offspring remained for several generations, then moved to Chemainus Bay. The story may have about it the unprovable aspect of legend but it cuts an intriguing linguistic trail. As late as the 1970s, a group of Natives in the Chemainus area were referred to as Xelaltxw—the Painted Houses—though by then the ancient village site and burial ground were long hidden under homes, a hotel and a pancake house.

The identity of the first white man to enter the Duncan area of the Cowichan people's homeland is unknowable. Maybe it was an inquisitive marine from Spaniard Francisco Eliza's 1791 expedition into the Strait of Georgia; maybe it was the Hudson's Bay Company trader John Work, who mentions the "Coweechin River" in his journals of 1824–27. Regardless, travellers had no appreciable effect on the Cowichans' lives. Missionaries, prospectors, government agents came and went, but until the settlers arrived, life in the valley cycled, as always, to the thirteen moons of the Cowichans' calendar, from winter's "a little ice on water" to autumn's "wind shakes down leaves."

The dull crack of a surveyor's axe on a transit peg signalled the end of Native dominance of the Cowichan Valley. In 1858, the Royal Engineers of the British Admiralty surveyed the area, cleaving it into 40-hectare sections. Some Cowichans resented the intrusion and chased the surveyors away with hatchets, but the engineers persisted. They set aside several hundred hectares along the river and marked it on their charts as Indian Reserve No. 1. The boundary extended as far north as Strawberry Hill and included the villages of Quamichan, Somena and the encampment called Siyaykw. The Natives were told the lands outside the reserve were for settlement but lands inside were for them to use as they pleased—hunting, fishing, building longhouses.

In September 1862, Siyaykw and 80 hectares of land around it were sold to Alexander Munroe for £200. Munroe was actually an agent; he made the purchase for relatives in Ontario. When the paperwork was complete he arrived at the entrance of a longhouse and knocked, then told the residents they had to move. The residents refused. Munroe returned with a constable at his side and asked the Natives to remove their buildings, their belongings and themselves. Again, he was refused. Over the next few years, Munroe learned the Cowichans were never informed he had purchased the area, nor had they received payment. In 1877 he wrote to the government: "after the lapse of so many years, I am convinced, as all must be who know the Indian character and will duly consider the facts of the case, that the only permanent and proper settlement will be by conceding the Indian right to the land and restoring it to them." His request was denied by the Department of Indian Affairs legal division, which claimed such a move would set a poor precedent and encourage other Natives to lobby for alienated lands. Munroe eventually gave up and the property was taken over and subdivided by two men with strong connections to the land in question. William Lomas was the Cowichan Indian Agent (and prohibited from purchasing Indian land according to the 1876 Indian Act) and Ashdown Henry Green was the original surveyor. The last Native residents of Siyaykw, the Sinametza family, were still claiming the land when they were evicted in 1893.

Such land disputes were part of the Cowichan Valley's so-called Indian Problem. An Indian Problem could be a weir that interfered with a sport fisherman's favourite run, or it could be a patch of Native-grown corn trampled by a settler's cow. There was a time when settlers believed the Indian Problem would be solved by disease. Smallpox, introduced not long after the establishment of Fort Victoria in 1849, devastated coastal Native communities. From an already diminished population of between 3,000 and 4,000 in 1862, the Cowichans were reduced in several years to 1,000. By 1900 they numbered just 500. Disease carried away the elderly and with them many traditions. The sick

A river journey west from Duncan around the turn of the century meant traversing Skutz Falls. Note the bucked log in the background— evidence of early log drives on the Cowichan River. BCARS A-07230

and dying were unable to bury the dead and many great longhouses at Somena and Quamichan became vacant.

The plight of Natives has been interpreted as the inevitable result of a primitive culture coming in contact with a more developed European one. Robert Brown thought otherwise. Brown was a strong-headed twenty-one-year-old Scot who had come to Vancouver Island to collect seeds for the Botanical Association of Edinburgh. He was fired from the appointment but found work as head of the government-funded Vancouver Island Exploration Expedition, which reported on the island's affairs—everything from botany to rocks, hydrology to Native population. In June 1864, the expedition boarded a steamer in Victoria and travelled to Cowichan Bay. There Brown hired Native canoemen to take them up the river. The journey along the river's lower reaches took several days. At Somena, Brown squatted in the shade of a cottonwood to talk with the village chief. Kakalatza, an elderly gentleman who smoked a straight-stem pipe and wore a stovepipe hat, had once fished the river from lake to bay. Old age now kept him at home. When Brown asked Kakalatza where the village's warriors had gone, the chief gestured into nearby bushes, where carved figures marked a cluster of graves.

Unlike many contemporary observers, Brown identified the hypocrisy in government policy that demanded Native loyalty to the Queen yet offered none of the benefits of citizenship. "The Indians have not been treated well by any means," he scrawled in his journal one evening. "There is continually an empty boast that they are British subjects, but yet have none of the privileges or the right of one." On the second night of the expedition, Brown and his fellow travellers camped on the banks of the Cowichan River near the present site of Duncan. "A lovely place embosomed by alders" is how he described the area. That evening he had a conversation with a Native that seemed, for Brown, the best articulation of Native/non-Native relations. "You came to our country," the Cowichan told him.

> We did not resist you—you got our women with children & then left them upon us—or put them away when they could have no children to keep up our race... You brought diseases amongst us which are killing us. You took our lands and did not pay us for them. You drove away our deer & salmon & all this you did & now if we wish to buy a glass of firewater to keep our hearts up you will not allow us. What *do* you white men wish?

What William Duncan and the other settlers wanted was land: free of Indians, fenced, thick with crops. The era of the mixed farm was at its height in the 1860s; with luck and hard work a man could reasonably expect to make a living off 40 arable hectares. If he could entice a woman to join him, they might actually prosper. Inspired by memories of well-tended farmland in Ontario and England, the settlers who came to Cowichan were determined to transform forest into field and paddock.

The Duncan area was pre-empted by five parties. What is now the Cairnsmore Street region was claimed by British-born Reverend David Holmes, an ordained deacon in the Church of England. Athletic and energetic, he had served at Yale, BC, where he built three churches and mastered two local Native languages so thoroughly that he was able to alternate between both in his sermons. Holmes built a large wedding-cake manor, Holmesdale, on the future College Street and set about establishing no fewer than four churches: at Somenos, Quamichan, Westholme and Chemainus.

To the south and east of the Holmes pre-emption, the Evans brothers had

a large parcel. Founders of the valley's widespread Evans clan, John, David and James had come to Cowichan from Wales in 1862. John and James were foot-loose, but David remained and built a cabin at the southwest corner of the claim (later the corner of First Street and Canada Avenue). When James returned from his travels David sold him the whole farm for $150. It extended from the bottom of Hospital Hill to the present site of the Trans-Canada Highway. To the east of the Evans property was the pre-emption of David and Margaret Alexander, including some of the best land in the valley. To the south of their property was the *in absentia* Munroe claim.

Bracketed between these claims and the Cowichan Reserve was William Duncan's rectangular pre-emption, marked as Section 17, Range 6 on survey maps and later defined by Boundary Street to the west and the Trans-Canada Highway to the east. This area would become the centre of the city.

Like his pioneering neighbours, William Duncan faced a dilemma of priorities. A settler needed shelter but he also needed a rudimentary barnyard for

In the Beginning ——————————————————

If the Duncan area's first inhabitants were ultimately from "somewhere else," so too was the land. Below the alluvial soils on which the city is built lies a massive rock shelf formed from a series of volcanic eruptions south of the equator 370 million years ago. The Wrangellia terrane, as it is called, drifted northward among the earth's plates at a millimetres-per-millennium speed until it came to a geological thud against the westerly moving North American continent. It in turn was rammed by other rogue terranes, thereby creating the unique train-wreck structure of southern Vancouver Island geology.

That's the big picture. The details of the Cowichan Valley's profile owe more to the glaciers and the Cowichan River. Starting two million years ago, a series of ice sheets emerged from the island's mountainous interior and inched southeast. Working like sandpaper on rough-cut lumber, they rounded the valley's sides and bottom and created the open book U-shape. The last of these ice sheets, the Fraser Glaciation, was so heavy that it depressed the earth's surface below sea level. For several thousand years the valley teemed with fish. When the Fraser Glaciation retreated, starting 15,000 years ago, the area rebounded. At the same time, glacial meltwater freighted the valley bottom with the rich sedimentary deposits that make it such fine agricultural land.

Compared with the forces of rock and ice, the Cowichan River seems more like a tuning fork than an instrument of large-scale topographical transformation. Yet time and the infinite power of running water wrought change. Before it was dyked and channelled in the 1880s, the Cowichan was, literally, a Hydra-headed force roaming freely over the eastern end of the valley, including what is now City of Duncan territory. Spring freshets often sent an arm of the river freelancing away from the main channel, carving new paths in the lightly packed sediments and buckling around areas of dense aggregate. Geologists believe it was such a scenario that created two of Duncan's more prominent features: the tree-covered mound south of Government Street known as Strawberry Hill and the block-and-a-half-long ridge between Brae Road and Duncan Street where William Duncan built his home. As recently as the 1850s, the Brae Road mound was bordered by a snaking arm of the Cowichan River, which brought ducks, trout and salmon to the city's south border. And to the east of Brae Road, between St. Julian Street and the Trans-Canada Highway, a river-created gully remained until the 1940s.

A similar but more ancient deviation in the river's course also created the bluff on the town's west and north sides. What was once a tree-lined bank of the Cowichan River now distinctly separates the benchland neighbourhoods of Centennial Heights and Buena Vista from the rest of the city.

pigs and poultry. He needed a well and a garden. If he used oxen, which great-
ly sped land clearing, he required pasture. Many valley areas needed draining.
Then, too, there was demand for trails so a man could make his way through
the forest to the steamer stop at Maple Bay and fetch supplies. Everything
needed doing and it needed doing all at once.

*The James Evans cabin, built
in the 1860s, was typical of a
"Bachelor's Hall." The building stood at the west end of
the family property at the
corner of what became First
Street and Canada Avenue.
CVM 987.6.1.1*

Most settlers started with a lean-to shelter. In the nearby forest they felled
timber in every direction for more than a tree length, so that the centre of the
clearing was beyond the reach of the tallest windfall. In this area they constructed a log cabin. A settler's first cabin was always called Bachelor's Hall.
William Duncan's Bachelor's Hall was about where Ypres Street intersects
Trunk Road. Other settlers thought it luxurious because the walls were hewn
on both sides instead of just one. All cabins were built from plans settlers carried in their heads, but they were remarkably similar. Usually about 3 metres
wide and 5 metres long, they were low-walled, built of logs chinked with mud,
and capped with a roof of hand-split cedar shakes. At one end was a door with
a low lintel and at the other a fireplace built of fieldstone and puddled clay. An
iron bar was fixed to the fireplace and from it hung a hook. A large cast-iron

pot swung from the hook and into it went venison, duck, goose, quail, salmon, trout, edible camas and watercress. Grouse and grouse eggs were a favourite meal. So were beans and bacon—poured over flapjacks they were known as "deadshot." In one corner of the cabin was a shakedown of straw under a three-stripe Hudson's Bay blanket and in another corner was an axe-hewn table graced by two primitive chairs. Between these simple furnishings there was just enough room for a slim man to manoeuvre.

The cabin was the settler's base. Each morning, often before dawn, he emerged to advance his claim. Chores first, then the interminable land clearing. A visitor passing by William Duncan in 1865 or '68 or '72 would have seen the same picture: a man with his shirt sleeves rolled up, inscribed in the flashing arc of an axe. The forest was the enemy. It had to be beaten back. Settlers in the Duncan area were more fortunate than their high-ground counterparts in that alder and maple covered much of the area. Hardwoods were easier to deal with than conifers. Felled in a pick-up sticks jackpot, they were chopped into lengths. (Functional bucking saws were not available until the 1880s.) The stumps remained in the ground; grass and crops were seeded by hand around them. When the logs on one claim had dried, settlers from surrounding claims arrived to help with the burning. Such events were called work bees and were later remembered as the most enjoyable of settlers' tasks. Men working behind one team of oxen competed with men working behind another team of oxen to see who could build the largest pyre. Afterwards, they feasted on roast pork or beef, freshly slain for the occasion. Then they returned to work their own claims.

A largely solitary life of hard work was dangerous to both spirit and body. A document found at the turn of the century recorded that 25 percent of the deaths in Cowichan in the late 1800s were work-related. According to the Register of Births, Deaths, Marriages and Cattle Brands, many fatalities were from falling trees and branches. Gunshot wounds killed settlers, as did bone-snapping kicks

"Few will develop the noble traits of the pioneers," wrote John Newell Evans, settler and historian, "for they will not be called upon to go through the same experiences which shaped our pioneers."
CVM 998.07.1.7

A Recipe for Bees

"All the settlers was dead broke," was how John Newell Evans often began his recollections of pioneer life in the Cowichan Valley. A friend of William Chalmers Duncan and later a long-time Municipality of North Cowichan alderman, the bushy-bearded Evans was also a prolific amateur historian, recording everything from the settlers' dietary favourites (potatoes cooked in their jackets) to the choicest wood for retoothing a harrow (crabapple). In a speech in the 1920s when he was in his sixties, Evans described the settlers' work bees—the co-operative efforts by which they helped each other clear land, build cabins and harvest crops.

First you would go into the woods and cut a big supply of hand spikes and skid poles to roll up your logs. Then you would set the date for your bee, and all your neighbors would answer your call.

There never was no lack of men. You usually got two yoke of oxen, and divided your crew into two parts, appointing a captain for each. Then the rivalry would commence, to see which team could pile the most logs.

Then we had raising or building bees, for bear in mind, there were but two saw mills operating; at Mill Bay and on the South side of Esquimalt Harbour. Most of the lumber used was whip-sawed at home, and you may say that running a whip-saw was a bee on a small scale. When you run a whip-saw, you have to have a pit. One man stands above the pit and takes the other end of the saw. The man that helped you got no pay; you returned his labour later.

All our buildings were of logs, cut in the Spring when the sap was running in the trees. You would bark your tree as you cut it down, when it is more easily barked, for if left unbarked on the ground for a very few days, you would have to chip off all the bark with your axe. For foundations, you would haul in large boulders on a stone boat.

Your neighbors would assemble early, and you would select the four best axe men as your corner men, for notching the corners. Even in those days, there were good axe men and poor axe men. The ground men rolled up the logs on skid poles to the corner men. When the building got too high, the corner men would tie ropes to the last log and pass the bight down to the ground men, who put the log in the bight. The corner men would haul on the ropes, while the ground men helped roll the log up as far as they could reach, then pushed with pike poles until the log reached the top of the wall. The roof was rafters and ribs of good straight poles, covered with split cedar shakes, split by hand with a froe.

On harvesting bees, it was a pretty sight to see half a dozen men going down a field, keeping in perfect time together in the swing of their scythes...The thrashing was done with a flail, which we in the early days dubbed "the poverty stick."

from horses. Even domestic chores were risky: the register's first entry is of a young girl who choked to death on a crabapple; the second is of an infant who died when scalded by hot water. Death came all ways. Historian Elizabeth Norcross tells the story of a young settler who broke his leg. He crawled from his cabin to the junction of two trails where he was found and carried on a stretcher to Cowichan Bay. He was taken by canoe to Saanich and by cart to Victoria. Exhausted from the travelling, he died several days later.

Adorning the settlers' simple life were a few social events, such as St. Peter's Spring Tea or the Cowichan and Saltspring Fall Fair, established in 1868 to showcase local agricultural goods. At these get-togethers settlers talked about farming or the perpetually off-schedule Maple Bay steamer and, if they were fortunate, met an eligible woman. There was such a scarcity of European women in BC

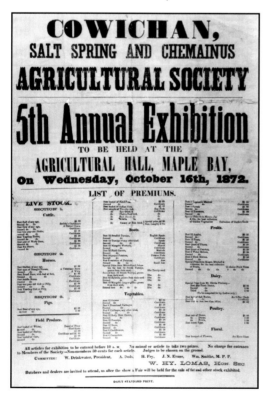

Top: Duncan-area settlers faced a full day's journey to fetch supplies from Maple Bay. Steamers were notoriously late—hence the corral for storing animals.
BCARS HP54515 B-3409

Left: BCARS 3751

that a society was formed to send out single females from Britain. Few of these beskirted emigrants made it beyond the bachelor-crowded docks in Victoria. One who did was Sarah Annie Ingram. Born on a farm in Donegal, Ireland, in 1845, Ingram was a bird-like woman with a frail body and quick, see-all eyes. When she was twenty-seven, Sarah and her sister Isabella came to BC. On the journey across the Atlantic, Sarah mentioned to her fellow passengers that she was bound for Vancouver Island. No one on board had heard of such a place.

St. Peter's Church, Quamichan, was built by William Chalmers Duncan and Harry Evans, a coffin maker. Drawing by Ken Hicks

At first the sisters lived in Victoria; when Isabella married Charles Todd they all moved to Saanich. Todd, as it happened, had worked in the goldfields with William Duncan. On a chance steamer excursion to the Cowichan Fall Fair in 1872, the threesome ran into Duncan, who had just walked four hours from his claim to eye the local produce but was still energetic enough to impress Sarah. After a suitable courtship he proposed. The two were married in 1876 in Victoria's St. John's Iron Church and left immediately for Duncan's farm: "We had breakfast and then went on board the steamer for Maple Bay," Sarah recalled years later, "and that was the beginning of my life in the bush."

Sarah Annie Ingram transformed William Duncan's life in the way a lace doily graces a barren table. William Duncan always had the dour Scots in him; a November-rain seriousness affected everything he did. Sarah, in comparison, saw pretty patterns in her tea leaves, had a bit of the fay about her and was relentlessly cheery. She was not a physically powerful woman and steadfastly refused to accept dawn-to-dusk labours as the necessary fate of a pioneer homemaker. On the day she arrived at William Duncan's cabin, she dragged a hard-backed chair to an east-facing window and positioned it where she could see Mt. Tzouhalem. Her travelling days were done, she said. For the rest of her life Sarah Duncan never ventured more than a few miles from the home. She bore seven children, did chores and needlework, read voraciously, lived long. (In her late eighties she was still scything thistles and at eighty-nine, in 1933, she was reading travel books. "Sometimes," she told a reporter, "I wonder why people live so long.")

A Trunk Road view of William and Sarah Duncan's home, Alderlea, c. 1900. CVM 989.10.2.5

With Sarah looking after the house, William Duncan was able to devote himself to the farm, which was to the east of their Brae Road home. He planted an apple orchard and brought in dairy cattle. He grew raspberries and vegetables. Long rows of strawberries ran down the slopes from his house: Warfields, Wilsons and plum-sized Sharpless, for which he took firsts at the Cowichan Horticultural, Dog and Poultry Show. His stable was the envy of neighbouring settlers, his alfalfa dense and sweet. His fields were thick with corn, wheat and splendid crops of oats that grew head high. "Mr. Duncan believes in general farming, even to bee keeping," wrote an admiring visitor to the farm. "[He] is a very careful man and very methodical in his habits; everything is done by routine so that when he goes in the house at night he can rest, for the day's work has been well and regularly done, everything having been properly looked after."

Duncan's Crossing

IF THE COWICHAN VALLEY had developed like other West Coast communities, William Duncan's farm would be still intact and Maple Bay would be an urban centre. Maple Bay was the port; through it goods and people were shipped. Typically, ports attracted business, business attracted settlement. That's how it worked in Nanaimo, Ladysmith, Port Alberni and Campbell River. The Cowichan Valley developed otherwise because of the curious historical confluence of two personalities: an obscure road foreman remembered only as Titus, and the larger-than-life Canadian Prime Minister, Sir John A. Macdonald.

The long slow boil of history has left but a residue of Titus. There are no known photos of him, nor any letters or documents. Was he lantern-jawed? Chinless? Loquacious? Tight-lipped? Did he live in a brick house with a rose garden in front, a tabby cat on the couch and children thumping on the wood

The railway bridge over the Cowichan River, c. 1911. The railway replaced the east-west river corridor with north-south access to Victoria and Nanaimo. CVM 980.04.1.11

floor overhead? Swallowed whole by history, his life remains unknowable. Of Titus's (presumably) average life only two things are known for sure. He was from Victoria. He was an awful road builder.

Starting in the early 1870s, the provincial government awarded a series of road construction and maintenance contracts for the Cowichan Valley. Many of these contracts went to Titus. Every summer he arrived via the Goldstream Trail with a gang of labourers and teams of oxen. They shaled roads, cut grades, cleared brush and bridged creeks. His work looked fine—until the winter rains set in. By then he was back in the capital. Low-lying areas turned to impassable pudding, switchback trails folded in on one another like a Chinese fan. Freshets washed away bridges. When Titus returned in the summer, the settlers told him of the problem spots but he refused to act on their suggestions. Each year the cycle repeated as immutably as the salmon runs: summer roadwork, winter transportation hassles, constant grousing.

Dissatisfaction with Titus's roadwork led in 1873 to the creation of the Municipality of North Cowichan—fourth-oldest municipality in BC and the political seed tree of the City of Duncan. The idea of incorporation was first suggested by William Duncan at a meeting of disgruntled settlers. North

Cowichan was a sprawling political entity covering the valley from the Cowichan River north to Chemainus. One of the municipality's first acts was to appoint pathmasters to oversee maintenance of local roads. They had a modest budget and, according to council minutes of February 1881, "full power to cause the work to be done in their districts when and where they deem fit." The pathmaster's chief resource was the statutory labour he could claim from any settler. Two days a year, between seedtime and harvest, farmers were recruited into road gangs. With their muscle, paths became trails, trails became roads. Better transportation made it possible for groups to attend meetings, private theatricals or special occasions, such as the visit, on August 13, 1886, of Sir John A. Macdonald.

Of Sir John A. perhaps a little too much is known. Accounts of his unslakable thirst for alcohol and his private tragedies threaten to eclipse his public accomplishments. In the context of Canadian history, August 13, 1886 is noteworthy as the day Macdonald tapped home the E&N Railway's last spike at Cliffside, near Shawnigan Lake. The 70-mile-long Nanaimo to Victoria railway was both the final link in Macdonald's sea-to-sea vision of a transcontinental railway and the fulfillment of a promise made to British Columbia more than a decade before, in return for joining Confederation. According to the day's itinerary, the prime minister and entourage (including Lady Macdonald and Robert Dunsmuir, the railway builder, and his wife Joan) were to board a train in Victoria and travel to Cliffside. After a quick ceremony they were to continue northward, stopping briefly at several settlements before arriving in Nanaimo.

Settlers in the Cowichan Valley, however, had no intention of letting the prime minister pass them by. Ever since BC had signed into Confederation, William Duncan and his neighbours had looked forward to an easy, quick way to ship milk and other farm produce to larger markets north and south. The settlers were originally told there would be three stations in the area: at Koksilah, Somenos and somewhere in the area of William Duncan's farm. Each was to be close enough to the clustered farms that no one was inconvenienced. The promise of a station inspired William Duncan to hire a surveyor, who laid out a townsite on the forested west side of the right-of-way, adjacent to the recently completed Trunk Road. He called his proposed settlement Alderlea.

When rail building had already commenced, the settlers around Duncan's Crossing (as it was becoming known) were advised that Robert Dunsmuir had determined there was not enough population to support a station; there would be no train stop at Duncan's. In the months between Dunsmuir's bad news and the visit by Macdonald, William Duncan canvassed the area for support for a station. He passed countless hours leaning on split-rail fences, talking in over-warm cabins, hollering down shafts to well diggers, arguing for the need to support a local station. As a direct result of his efforts, a crowd of several hundred people assembled on the morning of August 13 to meet the prime minister and the rail builder.

At 10:30 a.m., Macdonald's train chugged across the bridge that spanned the Cowichan River, and heaved to a stop under an arch of cedar and fir boughs erected by the settlers on Duncan's farm. As the crowd closed in around the train, a clutch of local students struck up a rendition of "Welcome to You All." Then a series of brief petitions were made: several Natives addressed the prime minister, followed by Indian Agent William Lomas and finally government agent Henry Fry, who gave a heartfelt speech on the pressing need for a station at that very spot. The crowning moment of the layover was when one of Lomas's daughters scrambled onto the train and thrust a bouquet of freshly picked flowers into Lady Macdonald's hand. Dunsmuir granted the settlers their wish.

That's the official version of Duncan's early genesis. Yet there is also a parallel account of Macdonald's visit. According to kitchen-table history, handed from settler to offspring and still heard in the valley, Macdonald and Dunsmuir yearned for day's end when the two could retreat from the prying eyes of wives and public into one of Dunsmuir's coal mines to sample aplenty the industrialist's cache of fine liquors. At Duncan's Crossing, speech led to speech until Dunsmuir foreshortened the petition by granting the locals their wish. Bouquet or booze—the result was the same. As Macdonald's train whistled its departure, Robert Dunsmuir, standing on the platform of the rear coach, lifted his stovepipe hat in farewell and shouted, "All right boys, you'll get your station."

In 1887, Dunsmuir's crews cleared brush from the west side of the railway tracks and put up a station. It was a long, low-walled structure that sat under such an enormous roof it looked like a child wearing an adult hat. Around the humble building a new settlement rose—not contiguously, but in a patchwork with a store here, a shop down the way, scattered cabins between.

One of the first to build was William Beaumont, the storekeeper who had hoped to transform Maple Bay into a town. Recognizing that Duncan's Crossing was destined to be the valley's commercial epicentre, he erected the Alderlea Hotel across the tracks from the station in the shadow of a landmark double-flowering dogwood. Soon afterwards Herbert Keast opened a livery stable. His building was down a muddy track supposed to be Station Street. Across from Keast, Robert Grassie started a smithy. A block north of the Alderlea Hotel, Frank Price built the Quamichan Hotel, an imposing, elegant structure that graced the squalor of the settlement's infancy.

The proprietors of these businesses were stalwart, conservative types who voted by tradition and wound their pocket watches at the same time every day; the early history of Duncan is remarkably free of itinerants and ne'er-do-wells. There was no gold to be found in Duncan, nor was there the quick-to-riches money in timber that would later launch several valley fortunes. Duncan was a

Duncan's Station and the Quamichan Hotel, 1888. William Duncan wanted to call the settlement Alderlea, but the railway insisted on Duncan's Station. The settlement was known as Duncan's Station, or Duncan's Crossing or Duncans, until incorporation in 1912 when it became the City of Duncan. CVM 989.10.2.10

The Alderlea Hotel, 1910. Sweat, tobacco juice and cigar smoke merged to created the Alderlea's distinctive atmosphere. CVM 984.34.2

place where a family invested their time and money and counted on it returning in the long run. The biographies of the first generation of merchants show remarkable similarities: a scandal-fuelled departure from the Old Country, a hard-scrabble beginning in the new land, a clenched-jaw determination to succeed.

William and Clara Jaynes were such a couple. The Jayneses opened the first general store in Duncan's, a whitewashed building with a great false front built kitty-corner to the station on Front Street. Painted across the building in enormous letters was "Jaynes," as if they were competing for business in a city miles wide. They sold domestic merchandise: flour and spices and tea, pan-head shovels, hand-forged nails, liniments—and things settlers couldn't make themselves. Like many early enterprises, their success was based on a partnership between man and wife—but not a traditional one.

The Alderlea Hotel: A Bit of the Wild West

A man looking for a drink in turn of the century Duncan had three establishments to choose from: the Quamichan Hotel on Duncan Street, where businessmen and commercial travellers gathered; the Tzouhalem Hotel at the corner of Trunk Road and Front Street, well fitted for the mint julep and cravat set; and the Alderlea Hotel at the brow of Duncan's Hill on Trunk Road. The Alderlea Hotel was where the working man drank. Box-like and partitioned with single-plank, cheese-hole walls, it was Duncan's equivalent to the raucous Mt. Sicker Hotel, or Lake Cowichan's fistworn Riverside: smoky, collegial, fight-ridden, noisy, overpriced, dirty, ugly, skunky; in short, a classic frontier-style bar.

In 1899, the Alderlea Hotel was leased to Charles Herbert Dickie, who was later a long-serving MLA and MP for the Cowichan Valley. Dickie, then forty-one years old, was a big, strong man with shoulders like roasts of beef and hands large enough to encircle a bottle of Scotch (which they regularly did). He had just been sacked by the E&N Railway for threatening to stuff an engineer into the firebox, and the Alderlea, with its low smog of cigar smoke and promise of lazy, yarn-filled afternoons, seemed to Dickie a near ideal way to make a living.

It wasn't. The first day Dickie was in charge he had to escort two men, still mounted on their horses, out of the bar. In the dining room, dissatisfied customers hurled tough steaks at Chinese waiters. While Dickie tended to a problem at one end of the building, inventory walked out a door at the other end. Clearly, he realized, the place was being run from "the wrong side of the bar."

Dickie's cleanup of the Alderlea started with the persistently troublesome customers. There was a long-armed fellow who filched cigars from a countertop case whenever the barman turned his back. Dickie removed one of the pricier stogies, tapped gunpowder into the core and returned it to the display. Then he stepped around a corner for a moment. "When I returned," recalled Dickie, "the gentleman in question was sitting by a window lighting a cigar; a moment after, his hat was blown off and the window was broken by the impact of his head." The proud hotelier observed a "slight increase in the profits derived from that branch of our trade operations."

Charles Herbert Dickie: MPP, MLA, railway fireman, hotelier, bouncer; c. 1900. Dickie family collection

Other troublemakers required a more traditional beer hall disposal. On a Monday afternoon an E&N trackwalker burst into the Alderlea and informed Dickie that a "big bad man," possibly carrying a pistol, was headed his way. Dickie retreated to a back room and worked out on the clubs and dumbbells. "To loosen up a little," he said.

The two met chin to chin over the Alderlea's shining hardwood bar. "My eyes sought a nice spot on his prominent jaw," recalled Dickie. The fellow made a threatening motion but Dickie was swifter. "I hit him where I looked and he went down and out. While removing him I went through his pockets but found neither weapons or money and I was sorry for hitting him so hard." The troublemaker was jailed and fined, but Dickie was so thankful for his absence he paid the fine.

Though he had the stern countenance of a classic late nineteenth-century industrialist, William Penn Jaynes was given to staring at the raindrops worming down his storefront windows and making introspective entries in his journal. He tended the accounts of the family business and was so famously tight with his money that a local wag immortalized his parsimony in verse:

> Mr Jaynes is the great lending merchant,
> His meanness cannot be described
> But I've heard people say
> He is just t'other way
> When some hookers of Scotch he's imbibed.

It was Clara Jaynes who had the entrepreneurial vigour. Clara was an attractive woman with a head of thick black hair and a distinctive just-woke-up squint that suggested skepticism. She was quick-tempered and could decide in a moment whether she liked someone or not. She also had a lifelong habit of sniffing that irritated some but which others found endearing. Of Clara's moods, Jaynes once wrote in his private journal that she was either "all honey or all shit."

The two met in England in 1870. William was a well-educated, handsome young man of twenty-four, training to take over his father's lumber business in London. Headstrong Clara Rhead had moved out of her mother's home rather than live with a dislikable stepfather, then shocked the class-conscious family by moving into a Gloucester hotel. Clara further scandalized her mother when it was rumoured she had taken a job as a barmaid. A striking young woman, an indomitable spirit, she attracted the attention of many men, including William Jaynes.

Clara was seventeen when she became pregnant. She lied about her age so she and William could get married. At first the couple kept their marriage a secret, but a maid discovered Clara's wedding ring under her pillow. The couple ran for Canada. They settled in Ontario, where William dug wells and Clara bore children. It was a difficult life, made more so when their house burned flat. On a tip—from Prime Minister John A. Macdonald, it is said, whom William knew through Conservative Party affiliations—the Jayneses travelled to Cowichan and chanced on a merchant willing to sell his general store. The enterprise was near the Quamichan Reserve and catered to Natives. When Duncan's Station opened, the couple built another store on Front Street (later Canada Avenue). The Jaynes partnership prospered—not in an exponential, boomtown way, for Duncan was never like that—but in a steady, year after year progression.

Prior to 1900, when the town's population figures hovered in the high double digits, the engine of this prosperity was agriculture. All around Duncan men were clearing land and planting crops. There seemed to be no end to what the valley's rich soils and warm wet climate would produce: tobacco, grapes, potatoes and especially grass. Thick, sweet grass grew nearly year-round in the valley, reducing the need to lay in huge crops for winter feed. The local climate was said to add $70 a hectare to the value of farmland. There were more dairy cattle in the Cowichan Valley than anywhere in BC except the Fraser Valley. Milk, cream and butter from cows fed on this rich pasture land was sought all over the island. It was the dairy industry, more than any other, that the railway opened.

In the years just after train service began, Cowichan dairy farmers drove into the station at Duncan's with their wax-papered blocks of butter and metal milk jugs for Victoria- and Nanaimo-bound trains. Farmers had their own contracts to supply certain stores and restaurants. The arrangement was problematic for both the retailer, who had to sell a product of inconsistent quality, and for the farmer, who had an extra burden of transforming milk into butter, then

William Penn Jaynes, diarist, father and pioneer merchant, c. 1921. CVM 989.1.5.1

delivering it. To address these problems, as much as anything, the Cowichan Creamery was established in 1895. Based on the then radical ideas of Professor R.W. Robertson, an Ontario Agriculture College dairy expert, the co-op dairy was the first of its kind in Western Canada. The co-op enabled Cowichan's farmers to share in the collective profit (or loss) of a season. More important, it standardized the industry, so that consumers could count on a product of generally consistent quality.

Though the creamery had the support of several top Duncan merchants—including the Jayneses—it was not a given that it would be built in Duncan. Farmers from Koksilah to Westholme lobbied to have the plant built close to their operations. A crucial factor in determining the creamery's placement was an abundant supply of well water. Test holes were dug at several proposed sites, including a lot just north of William Duncan's home. Where other holes oozed, the excavations on the Duncan lots rapidly filled with a fine, seemingly endless flow of teeth-chilling potable water.

In the first year, the Cowichan Creamery shipped 21,000 kilograms of butter. A warehouse was added to the single-storey, false-fronted structure, then a

Above: Old Country purebreds always did well at the Cowichan Fall Fair. These sheep were part of the 1910 exhibition. CVM 983.64.1

Right: The Cowichan Creamery with the James Evans farm and farmhouse in the background. Until blasting powder became available, in 1903, most settlers seeded around stumps. CVM 980.1.2.6

grain elevator. An egg sorting facility was tacked on. Flush with healthy dividends, members had all sorts of ideas for expanding the business. The creation of a farm machinery division worked; the installation of a piggery within whiffing distance of town did not. From a total original investment of $3,000 by seventy district farmers, the co-op grew eventually to a thriving firm doing $300,000 annually on behalf of 300 shareholders. It was the town's only legitimate factory and a signifi-

cant contributor of taxes. Rural families came into town to do creamery business then stayed for a meal or a theatrical production. For years the busiest business days in Duncan were Monday, Wednesday and Friday, the days when dairymen brought their milk to the creamery. Thursday was declared a half-day holiday, an acknowledgement by local merchants that the little town still cycled to the rhythms of the nearby farmland.

Duncans Station, E. & N. Rly., Vancouver Island, British Columbia. (Train arriving from the North.)

Top: Seasonal agricultural work fit in with traditional Native economy. This Native-operated threshing machine, photographed in 1916, was one of the first in the valley. CVM 988.08.2.43

Left: A southbound train arrives at Duncan's Station under the landmark pinnacles of S'wukus (Mt. Prevost), c, 1910. The railroad expanded its Duncan yard to five tracks to accommodate log and farm freight. CVM 988.03.5.1

A Bard's Training

Before venturing to the Yukon, where he wrote "The Cremation of Sam McGee" and the other ballads that would make him the world's best-selling poet, Robert W. Service was just another no-name British farm pupil in Duncan: taking milk to the creamery, fetching supplies from Jaynes Store and weeding nearby turnip fields. Actually, Service worked in the area twice: from 1896–97 at the Mutter family farm in Somenos and 1898–1903 at Corfield's Cowichan Bay estate.

Several biographers have dismissed this period in Service's life as uneventful, but the poet himself thought otherwise. In his 1945 memoir, *Ploughman of the Moon: An Adventure into Memory,* Service recalled Duncan as the place where he developed as an entertainer; discovered his hatred for manual labour; and was very nearly emasculated with a pitchfork. The latter misadventure happened in a barn just outside of town. One morning Service was assigned to a gang of farm workers weeding turnips. His co-workers included an attractive young woman named Minnie, whose strong features and luminous eyes, he recalled, "aroused my ardour." Minnie's boyfriend, Johnny Fat, was also in the field but his presence did nothing to stop Service from returning Minnie's occasional glances with winks and amorous smiles.

The courtship lasted half a day. At lunchtime, while the rest of the crew were eating, Service wandered into a barn and flopped onto a haystack. He was just drifting off to sleep when a pitchfork flashed into the hay beside his thigh and vanished to the helve. He scrambled up but could not see anything in the barn's darkened recesses. Still, Johnny Fat's message was clear. "After that," Service wrote, "I left his girl alone."

No matter how rough his job or low his spirits, Service always retained the fine manners and toney accent that opened doors to Duncan's high society. And it was in this society that he discovered a talent for entertaining. He started by singing in the choir at St. Peter's Anglican Church, then was persuaded to perform at Saturday night dances. He arrived at the dances riding a borrowed bicycle and packing a borrowed banjo. He played hard and rode home in the "pitchy dark," navigating by the roadways' pothole braille. Eventually Service joined a Duncan theatrical troupe and starred in such contemporary standbys as *The Area Belle, Ici on Parle Français* and *Box and Cox.* The productions were amateur but he took them seriously, memorizing lines while milking and rehearsing in front of a mirror. (He found it useful to take a single, bracing slug of Scotch just before stepping on stage.) Service himself acknowledged that his

Duncan-era performances were not stellar but they did inspire in the well-mannered farmhand a confidence that his real talents lay elsewhere.

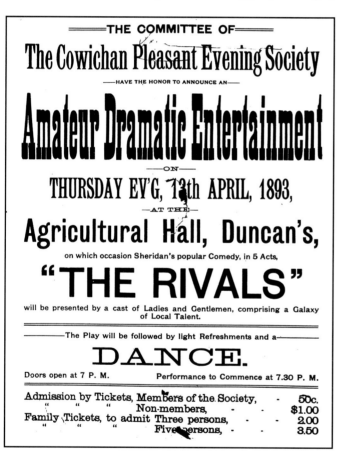

=THE COMMITTEE OF=

The Cowichan Pleasant Evening Society

—HAVE THE HONOR TO ANNOUNCE AN—

Amateur Dramatic Entertainment

—ON—

THURSDAY EV'G, 13th APRIL, 1893,

—AT THE—

Agricultural Hall, Duncan's,

on which occasion Sheridan's popular Comedy, in 5 Acts,

"THE RIVALS"

will be presented by a cast of Ladies and Gentlemen, comprising a Galaxy of Local Talent.

—The Play will be followed by light Refreshments and a—

DANCE.

Doors open at 7 P. M.   Performance to Commence at 7.30 P. M.

Admission by Tickets, Members of the Society,   -   50c.
    "   "   "   Non-members,   -   - $1.00
Family Tickets, to admit Three persons,   -   -   2.00
    "   "   "   Five persons,   -   -   3.50

Opposite & left: The poet Robert Service recalled in his later years that he first found expression for his acting abilities in Duncan's vibrant amateur theatre scene. CVM 994.02.9.2; BCARS PDP3443

Cheap Land, Fair Climate

WILLIE MCKINNON, the fourteen-year-old son of Mr. Angus McKinnon, underwent a most startling experience and had a miraculous escape from death on last Thursday morning. While working in his father's garden about half past eleven o'clock, a meteor about ten inches in diameter was hurled through space and buried itself in the ground about eight feet from where the boy was standing. The meteor could be heard coming for several minutes before it struck the earth, but the lad, thinking it was a train passing, took no notice until the celestial visitor struck the earth, sending the rocks flying in every direction and causing an effect like an earthquake in that vicinity.

—*Cowichan Leader*, September 5, 1908

They heard Harry Smith before he hit Duncan's, too. A great tremulous siphoning sound preceded his arrival, like an enormous rubber boot being pulled from gumbo. That's what they said later, anyway. But we always claim foreknowledge when it comes to events outside of our experience. And most assuredly, Duncan's had never experienced a Harry Smith.

Probably not a single Duncan's resident noticed the undistinctive Smith when he first passed through town in an E&N carriage, on a blue-sky spring day in 1897. With ebbing hairline, well-coiffed twenty-after-eight moustache and a leather case tucked between his knees, Smith resembled the typical travelling salesman, luggage crammed with self-sharpening knives or vials of impotency cures. As it happened, his bags contained a prospector's pick. And he was about to discover a mine that would change Duncan forever.

Prospector, retailer, developer, newspaperman, part-time huckster, full-time booster, Harry Smith was the exception to the generally stalwart cast of characters that made up the Duncan's business core in the late 1890s and early 1900s. Like Clara Jaynes and so many other merchants, Harry Smith was born in England; beyond that they were as different as salt water and fresh. Clara spent most of her life in steady work toward success and financial security; Harry Smith couldn't give a damn for security. For him, the pleasure was in the hunt. He liked wooing money, but once in his hands it vanished. He had a similar passion for getting enterprises going; when their success was ensured, his interest cooled. Smith figures prominently in so many initiatives that it would be quicker to list what he wasn't involved in than what he was.

Harry Smith, c. 1905.
CVM 997.3.4.2

Hard-working, hard-spending Mt. Sicker miners created their own town and fuelled growth in nearby Duncan.
BCARS C-08618

In the parlance of the day, Harry Smith was an "end of the rails man," a term applied to any chronically energetic, slightly desperate character in a new settlement who left a lamp lit should other opportunity come by for a visit. He was the youngest of thirteen children born to a Cambridgeshire tenant farmer, and he was still a boy when his family moved to Chicago. He decided to forgo formal education for tutorial in the working world and, at the age of twelve, signed on as a fireman on a Michigan railway. Later he hitched a ride on a westerly moving mule train and bumped and jarred his way across the still unsettled Great Plains. He lived on stump ranches all over Puget Sound, and through a political connection got a job as customs inspector. While working in Port Townsend, Washington, Harry Smith heard from friends about an ore-rich range of mountains on southern Vancouver Island. Henry Buzzard and F.L. Sullins had sweated away the summer of '96 prospecting Mt. Sicker, then abandoned the project still hopeful the area could yield paying ore. According to Harry Smith's internal clock, it was about time for an adventure.

With a prospector's hammer tucked in his leather case, Harry took a

steamer across Juan de Fuca Strait, then the train north to Chemainus. For three weeks he clambered around the fire-blackened slopes of Mt. Sicker. He ate from his skillet and drank from streams. On the mountain's west side he finally located a well-defined copper lead. Smith staked it in honour of his daughter, Lenora. The Lenora claim may have been remote but the kind of money attracted to mining investments in the late 1800s moved as swiftly as the fingers of the telegraph operators who tapped news of Smith's find around the world. Soon there were sixty claims blanketing the mountainside around Lenora, and by 1902 Mt. Sicker featured two functional mines, a railway, two hotels and the biggest settlement outside of Victoria and Nanaimo.

The growth of Mt. Sicker—explosion is a more appropriate term—had a vortex effect on Duncan's, dragging the sleepy agricultural town to a heightened prosperity. Three boom-town effects were written all over Duncan: in the fine cloth wares of the Bon Ton Millinery and the Imperial Gentleman's Furnishings, in the exotic vellum at Prevost's stationery shop, in the ornate wares at William Dobson's paint and paper store, in the round-the-clock,

Harry Smith's Duncan's Emporium building still stands in Duncan. It has housed a general store, a druggist, a clothing shop and Roland Thorpe's furniture store. Note the child in the foreground. CVM 995.11.6.22

cash-rich card games that went on in the smoky recesses of the Alderlea Hotel.

Leading the surge of those who saw opportunities in Duncan was Harry Smith himself. He swapped his mine owner's cap for a retailer's linen apron, moved to the settlement and opened Duncan's Emporium, an allsorts shop on the south side of Station Street that reflected its owner's diverse interests. He also tried storing dynamite in a Craig Street shack but that venture was nixed by nervous merchants. Smith moved the emporium to the northeast corner of Station and Craig Strets, then sold to Pitt and Peterson who, in turn, formed a partnership with the Jayneses to start Cowichan Merchants, for many years the largest retail building in BC outside of Victoria and Vancouver. Smith also started the Duncan's Opera House and was a founder of the Alderlea Fire Brigade, later the Duncan Volunteer Fire Department.

His most public contribution was no doubt the creation of the *Duncan Enterprise*, the settlement's first newspaper. Smith founded the paper when he went to advertise his Duncan's Emporium and found no newspaper existed. The paper debuted on January 21, 1900. "We can hardly call this a newspaper," said the editor in a massive understatement. The *Enterprise* had four sheets, measured 23 by 30 centimetres and featured the most recent news from the Boer War, articles on poultry sexing and tidbits of local news such as an item about a local horse named Bones that wandered into Charlie Grassie's forge whenever his corns became bothersome. Initially an all-Smith affair—it was written by Harry and distributed by his son Cornelius—the *Enterprise* ran for a year before it died. In 1905 Smith replaced it with the *Cowichan Leader*, then lit out for the north. He started the first stores in Stewart and Prince Rupert and mined in Alaska before heading south to get involved in market gardening and chrome mining in California. In the 1930s Smith retired to his son's Gibbins Road home, where he drank pension-paid rum and perused the *Leader* for stories about the town on which he had made such a remarkable impact.

The Cowichan Valley was still wilderness when a tragedy unfolded halfway around the world which was to have a belatedly profound effect on Duncan's. In the late 1850s, legions of smartly dressed British cavalry rose from the barricades on the Crimea Peninsula where their country was waging war with the Russian Army and, to the bellowed orders of their officers, spurred their mounts into the shredding gunfire of the enemy. Soldiers and steeds fell in rows as orderly and expansive as the British Empire they died for.

The Cowichan Leader

Before radio station CKAY, the *Cowichan News* and the *Pictorial* broke open the Duncan media market (in the 1960s and 1970s), the sole arbiter of public stories in Duncan was the editor of the *Cowichan Leader*. For sixty years the paper's various editors decided what was fit to print and, often more important, what wasn't. They had to balance the paper's duty to report fairly and honestly on issues of the day with its simultaneous need to exist in the community. As one beleaguered *Leader* editor put it, "Should an editor publish everything that some people would like to have him publish, he would be in jail half the time and in hospital the other half."

A pugnacious *Leader* editor was Edwyn Harry Lukin Johnston, known as Rufus to his family and Lukin to readers. His tenure at the newspaper coincided with the prosperous years 1911–14. Johnston was a well-educated, athletic Englishman who stumbled into the job after a brief career selling life insurance. At the time he started as editor, the *Leader* was being published from a Station Street office between Miss Baron's clothing store and The Tea Kettle Inn. The editor sat next to a backfiring gasoline engine that powered the paper's vintage 1830 Hoe Press, the same press that had been used to print the first copies of Victoria's *Daily Colonist* in 1858. Whenever the press ran, the building did the Charleston. The engine exhausted into the editor's face. The only good thing Johnston could find to say about the arrangement was that it "obviated the need for lunch."

Johnston was similarly unimpressed with the *Leader*'s journalistic content. The previous editor, F.A. Brettingham, was secretary to the Conservative Party and the paper reflected a Tory bias. Johnston announced that the paper was henceforth emphatically neutral. To emphasize his point he attacked the CPR—previously considered a corporate untouchable—for its shoddy train service, and sent copies of the paper to top CPR officials. The article so incensed the railway's local superintendent that he stomped into the *Leader*'s office and threatened to hammer the "insolent cub." Johnston called his bluff by offering to clear the office and settle the issue man to man.

Such high-octane journalism is ultimately unsustainable in a small town. Johnston's successful muckraking was his own undoing. In 1913 he was tipped that the provincial government was being lobbied to subsidize construction of a road to Cowichan Lake. The lobbyists were wealthy Victoria businessmen who would profit by the access. The group included Sam Matson, owner of the *Daily Colonist*. Matson offered the upstart reporter a lucrative job as night editor at a better salary and Johnston was plucked from Duncan.

The man who replaced Johnston, Hugh George Egioke Savage, was the paper's most successful editor and, later, owner/publisher. Part of this success was a function of his lengthy tenure. He was with the paper for forty-three years and brought a continuity that earned it several awards, including the 1928 Mason Trophy for the best weekly in Canada. For several generations of readers, Hugh Savage was the paper and the paper was Hugh Savage.

Round-faced, with a small mouth and closely cropped moustache, "Cougar Hughie," as he was known in journalism circles, came to Cowichan after a career with the Vancouver dailies, where he once helped track a renegade cougar in Stanley Park, then packed the dead cat out on his shoulders to break the story. With careful attention to detail, Savage transformed the *Leader* into one of the most successful small-town papers in Canada, fat with advertisements and with a Class A circulation. Under his patriarchal tutelage, the paper won the loyalty of Duncan's merchants by refusing to sell display advertising to out-of-town businesses, and of the entire population by getting their names in the paper—spelled correctly.

It did not hurt the *Leader*'s balance sheet that Savage's views on the Empire were in agreement with those of many British immigrants to Duncan. Under his tenure, for example, the paper ran recipes for royal wedding cakes ("12 lbs flour, 28 lbs Currants, 3 lbs Lemon Peel...") alongside more typical staples of small-town papers—unemployment rates, sports, local politics. A favourite Savage topic was the Oxford Group Movement, established in Britain, which encouraged its followers to absolutes of honesty, purity, love and unselfishness. The concept never caught on with the *Leader*'s pragmatic readers but that did not stop "Holy Hughie," as the less devout called him, from ensuring that the Movement got front-page coverage.

Hugh Savage sold the *Leader* in January 1957. He died one month later at age seventy-three.

Hugh George Egioke Savage, editor of the Leader *for forty-three years, in a drawing by Mort Graham, 1956.*

The Charge of the Light Brigade at Balaclava was one of the last great military paroxysms of Victorian England. Public outcry and shock at the slaughter permanently changed the British Army, for generations the refuge of the sons of England's upper class. Army reform meant that officer positions could

no longer be purchased; they had to be earned. Similar changes in the standards for law, medicine and even theology meant the doors to those formerly safe havens were shut too. Crowded out of England, the sons of wealthy gentry sought to create new lives in the great empty lands of the British empire: Australia, South Africa, New Zealand, Canada.

In the last quarter of the nineteenth century an estimated 45,000 gentlemen immigrants arrived in Canada from Great Britain. Some settled on the prairies, but most came west to the Lower Mainland and southern Vancouver Island where they took up farms and rural acreages or started businesses. No location attracted more of these gentlemen immigrants than the Cowichan Valley. Lured by cheap land, fair climate and the promise of blood sports, they settled around Duncan in clutches on Maple Bay Road, Quamichan Lake and at Somenos.

So began Duncan's era of the "Longstockings"—a generic term applied to almost all upper middle-class British emigrants, be they the so-called remittance

Harry Smith's one-man, one-boy operation became the Cowichan Leader, *honoured several times as one of Canada's finest small-town newspapers. Pictured above is the* Leader's *ferro-concrete printing plant, built in 1927. CVM 983.16.130*

men (basically, wayward sons paid to stay away); the farm students sent to the "Colony" to learn agriculture; or the ex-India Army officers whose meagre pensions prohibited retirement in the Old Country. The term originated with the emigrants' habit of wearing shorts and long puttees, often with mangled felt hats, elbowless tattery tweed jackets and sturdy boots, but it came to include those who displayed the social plumage of the upper class English. A Longstocking was, broadly, a man or woman of fine upbringing, often sporting a hyphenated last name, who was well schooled, enthusiastic about hunting and fishing, suspicious of the arts and mad about cricket. Eccentric, irritating and moneyed, they created what the writer Bruce Hutchison called a "peculiar civilization" around the little town.

Measuring the effect of this civilization on Duncan is like assessing the impact of garlic on a roast leg of lamb. The Longstockings flavoured the town without altering its substance. Economically, the city prospered on their stipends, remittances, or the pension cheques from the British Home Office and Admiralty that arrived at the post office every month. In the Depression of the 1930s, especially, when Longstocking population was at its peak, with more than 400 families and 1,500 individuals, their incomes propped up the town's ailing economy and so the shops never suffered the deprivations of cash-starved prairie towns. It was for the Longstockings' benefit that the shelves of Duncan's stores were stocked with English pipe tobacco, Eccles cake and the uniquely British concoction of lard and raisins called "spotted dick"; that Mann's drugstore called itself a chemist shop; that Westwell's stocked copies of *Field & Stream*, *Tatler* and *Sketch*; that the Tzouhalem Hotel served a curiously unCanadian breakfast: kippers and grilled kidney on toast.

In architecture, too, the Longstockings had definite tastes. Squirrelled down shady lanes and set amid clumps of oak trees, gorse bushes and forget-me-nots, the average Longstocking home was a sprawling, Tudor-style villa with a fireplace in every room and a double-barrelled shotgun over every mantle. They had names like The Maples, The Firs and The Bungalow. Many of these homes reflected what one observer called a "divided nostalgia" on the part of their owners: on three sides the fussy, lead-window ornamentation of English manors; on the sunny side a long verandah of the sort found in homes in Mandalay, Khartoum, Rawalpindi and other colonial outposts. The architect most successful in marrying these forms was Samuel Maclure—celebrated for designing the Dunsmuirs' palatial Hatley Park in Colwood, BC. Maclure's commissioned works around Duncan are still sought out by architecture aficionados.

Duncan's social life was transformed by the Longstockings. Where most pioneer communities had two distinct social groups—settlers and Natives—Duncan had three: the Longstockings, settlers (called short stockings) and Natives (called no stockings). Relations between Longstockings, who clearly saw themselves atop the social totem, and settlers were cordial but guarded. The average Duncan's-ite judged a man by his work, whereas the average Longstocking counted accent, social grace and adroitness with a croquet mallet as necessary requisites. The Canadian-born—or mossbacks, as Longstockings referred to the settlers—were uneducated and work-driven. Canadians called the Longstockings remittance men, or brass hats, namby-pambys, and told apocryphal-sounding stories about their levels of uselessness. One concerned a moneyed Englishman who purchased a local dairy farm for a small fortune. Six months later he sold out at a great loss, having belatedly discovered that the "damned cows had to be milked every day." Another story referred to a nameless tweedy Englishman who died of thirst at river's edge. Too fastidious to use his hands, he had perished for want of a cup.

The Tzouhalem Hotel's opulence appealed to Duncan's gentlemen immigrants—the so-called Longstockings, or Brass Hats. Pictured here in 1908 are Edith and Frank Price and their son Fred. CVM 993.03.2.1

Those and similar accounts transformed "Longstocking" into such a pejorative that the term retains its potency to this day. And that is unfortunate, because the Longstockings included some remarkable characters.

The most prominent of the first generation of gentleman immigrants to settle in the Duncan area was Sir Edward Clive Oldnall Long Phillipps-Wolley, diplomat, lawyer, soldier, sportsman, writer and one-time champion British amateur heavyweight boxer. Tall and angular with a messianic beard, he was

"THE GRANGE" 1912

Phillipps-Wolley's The Grange, outside Duncan's, 1912, in a drawing by Ken Hicks.

the embodiment of a Gilbert and Sullivan operetta. After serving as Her Majesty's Consul at Kertch in the Crimea, he practised law at Oxford's Middle Temple, then obtained a commission in the British Army and rose to the rank of captain. He was an avid hunter and boasted trophy kills on five continents. In 1897, at the age of forty-three, he moved to Victoria and wrote a series of books on big game hunting, patriotism and adventure. *Songs of an English Esau, A Sportsman's Eden* and *The Chicamon Stone* lodged Phillipps-Wolley among the top half-dozen of Canada's contemporary writers. Several years later he moved to Cowichan and had Samuel Maclure design a massive black and white, wood and stucco manor on Drinkwater Road, several kilometres north of Duncan. The Grange, as it was called, was Phillipps-Wolley's home for over a decade.

Like many other Longstockings, Phillipps-Wolley did not come to Cowichan to build a new culture but to re-create an old one. He lined the walls of The Grange with the mounted heads of elk, bear, cougar, caribou, wildebeest, lion, jaguar and tiger, hosted tea parties and wrote hymns to the royalty. His vision of British hegemony, articulated in poem and prose, was more spiritual than material. He saw British Columbia as a strand in the "organic whole" of the British Empire, and the men who defended it he said responded to a "voice" of loyalty. He identified many threats to his beloved "Empah" and, while in Duncan, set his crosshair sights on two, however incongruous: the rise of the Imperial German Navy and the efforts of Duncan motorists to have rules of the road changed from driving on the left (British) side to the right (American) side. The first threat Phillipps-Wolley countered by founding a western division of the Navy League of Canada, a lobbying organization that ultimately prompted the federal government to create a national navy. The situation on the roads he attacked via the *Cowichan Leader*. "Just one word of protest," he wrote the paper's editor. "You write in your last issue that it's not important whether we keep the English or the American rule of the road in B.C.—I venture to think it is . . . why should we learn new rules to please foreigners? One of the charms of the district for which you write, Mr. Editor, is that it is essentially British. Long may it remain so."

Phillipps-Wolley wasn't the only Longstocking whose notoriety helped earn Duncan's the title "The Most English Town in Canada." Duncan's could boast that Negley Farson had based his novel *The Story of A Lake* on valley characters he met during his brief residence. Rosamond Marshall, whose novel *Kitty* was a bestseller, lived nearby. So did Doctor Charles Stoker, brother of Bram Stoker, author of *Dracula*. Lon Chaney's brother George could often be seen pottering in town, clad in the worn, loose-fitting woollens that were a virtual Longstocking uniform.

A Victoria journalist once bet a visiting Winnipeg colleague a bottle of Scotch that within moments of arriving in Duncan they could identify a true Longstocking by dress alone. At that time it was said you could greet any shabby grey-hair on a Duncan street with "Hello, Colonel" and be right 99 percent of the time.

> On the first street we found a man in khaki shorts and the invariable tweed coat. My friend from Winnipeg began to look interested. Down the next street strode a lovely Colonel Blimp, with fly hooks all over his tweed hat. My friend gazed at him with innocent prairie admiration. And on my honor, with sworn evidence to support it, we found in the liquor store an old English gentleman in shorts, six inches of cotton drawers, and those long shiny boots that the Life Guards wear on sentry duty at Whitehall. My Winnipeg friend capitulated and bought the whiskey.

The old English gentleman in question was Captain Arthur Lane, a gap-toothed, slope-shouldered flag-bearer for all that was fripperous about the town's immigrant upper crust. Except for a brief stint overseas in the First World War and an ongoing sub-career as an anti-prohibitionist, Lane devoted his life to recreation: duck hunting, polo, cricket, or tooling around local waterways in his various yachts. He was the sort of fellow about whom others say "great fun," or "good sport." Lane was always up to an adventure, whether it was grubbing a boulder from his estate, Stoney Patch, on Quamichan Lake, or journeying to Calgary for a polo tournament. He loved gadgetry and was one of the first valley residents to get a telephone. Yet for all his levity there was something studied about Lane's eccentricities. His tattery clothes were Savile Row quality; his flamboyance was tempered by boys' school manners, such as sipping soup from the side of the spoon. As was the case with many Longstockings, there was orthodoxy in Lane's nonconformity.

Lane's foremost passion was for dress-up parties which in some loose way may have been linked to a celebrated event in the annals of the Lane family. In 1651, Mistress Lady Jane Lane single-handedly preserved the British monarchy by persuading the besieged King Charles II to dress as a manservant and accompany her on horseback past the army of the execution-minded Oliver Cromwell. The Royal forces eventually triumphed, of course, and the Lane family was thereafter granted a hefty annual stipend. In Duncan's, Arthur Lane honoured the legacy of his illustrious ancestor with legendary all-night bashes based on themes of the Old West, Mississippi riverboats, pirates and Indian mystics.

An aspect of Cowichan Valley life that Lane and other Longstockings took seriously was cricket. During the 1920s and 1930s the Cowichan cricket team's

fame extended throughout the Dominion. The side was so good that in 1932 the Australian test match team, on its way to England, stopped off for a game. This is akin to the World Champion Soviet Red Army hockey team of the 1980s dropping by to play the in-house team at the Crofton Pulp Mill. The Australians and the Cowichan team played in front of a thousand spectators on a sunny Friday at the Recreation Ground, between Wharncliffe Road and the river. The visitors were such ferocious hitters that children and dogs were prohibited from the sidelines. Even so, Kathleen Jobling had her tibia fractured by an errant ball hit by an Australian.

Top: The many versions of Captain Arthur Lane, c. 1910. Left to right: CVM 991.4.5.32p31 (4); 991.4.5.32p50 (3); 991.4.5.32p76 (4); 991.4.5.32p77 (6);

Left: Charles II, seated ahead of Lady Jane Lane (an ancestor of Arthur Lane) and disguised as her manservant, escapes from Cromwell's forces in 1651. Arthur Lane had a passion for period costume.

Arthur Lane and his Longstocking cohorts celebrated Victoria Day 1906 with cricket at Maple Bay beach, then adjourned to the nearby Elkington Estate for leapfrog. Another attraction was the South Cowichan Lawn Tennis Club, the oldest grass court club in the world besides Wimbledon.
Top: CVM 991.4.5.59p50 (1); bottom: CVM 991.4.5.59p50 (3)

The Australian side demolished the locals. That was expected. But the real sensation of the day was the failure of the great Australian batsman, Sir Don Bradman ("the batting wonder of the age") to make his customary century—one hundred runs. Bradman was at sixty when a British-born local farmer Geoffrey Baiss, star of the Cowichan side, bowled to him. Bradman deftly hit to his front and drove the leather ball straight down the pitch. Baiss made a magnificent move and caught the ball with a palm-splitting smack heard around the field. He held on and the great Bradman was out. At the time Baiss was in his fifties; he continued to play cricket for another twenty years.

When they were not playing dress-up or cricket, many Longstockings could be found along the banks of the Cowichan River, where they worked the runs of steelhead and trout with their great split-cane bamboo fly rods. Their

wicker creels and fly-garnished hats re-created scenes found on the legendary rivers of England and Scotland. Such a comparison was fine with Ashdown Henry Green. Born in Grosvenor Square, London and educated at Charterhouse, Green was bound for India when a doctor recommended he settle in the more moderate Pacific coast environment. His work in BC contradicts the notion that Longstockings were layabouts. He was smart, tough and tireless. He surveyed for the CPR and Department of Indian Affairs in areas never before seen. "I know the province like a book," he declared. Green settled in Duncan on 4 maple-strewn hectares along the banks of the Cowichan River. His home, later part of the Silver Bridge Inn, boasted a magnificent garden and a manicured tennis court (later washed away by the river).

Kilninta, as it was called, often echoed with the hymns of a St. Peter's Church choir practice or the Mayfair accents of fellow Longstockings who attended Green's lavish dinner parties. Mary Marriner, a Cowichan resident, describes a typical bash in her diary, New Year's Day 1897: "About fifty people were there. The house outside was prettily lit with Chinese lanterns which were hung on the veranda. Coffee, claret cup and cakes were served in the drawing room and more substantial refreshments in the dining room. Old Mr.

The Cowichan Cricket Club of 1912 at the Recreation Ground (later McAdam Park). The team included Geoffrey Baiss, whose catch against a visiting Australian test match team was still being discussed in the 1950s. Back row (left to right): Lukin Johnston, C.W. Johnson, Seymour Green, J. Hirsch, A. Thornton, MPP W.H. Hayward, Ruscombe Poole, C. Brooke-Smith, W.W. Bundock, H.F. Prevost, F. Young, W. Morten. Second Row: H. Hornibrook, R. Ashby, H. Charter, E.W. Carr-Hilton (Captain), W.A. McAdam, G.G. Baiss, H.B. Hayward. Front Row: Basil Carr-Hilton Jr., V. Knox, Douglas Carr-Hilton Sr., E. Stilwell. CVM 983.16.13b

Haynes played the violin and Mrs. Green the piano for the dancing…"

But Green was most content on and in the nearby river. He knew the Cowichan better than any non-Native of his day and was often consulted by fisheries officials. An enthusiastic ichthyologist, Green identified nine types of fish previously not found in BC waters, including two that took his name, the lake chub (*Couesius greenii*) and the lobefin snailfish (*Polypera greenii*). His collection of preserved fish became the nucleus of the fish exhibits at BC's provincial museum. For many years, one of his favourite flies—the Ashdown Green—graced packs of Sportsman cigarettes.

Offspring of what Gwladys Downes, a Duncan High School teacher, called the local "tiger skin rug crowd" had celebrated careers, too: Philip Livingstone (later Sir, KBE, CB, AFC, FRCS, DPH, DOMS, KHS), the son of Mt. Sicker mine manager Clermont Livingstone, pioneered RAF night-vision techniques and Colonel L. Oldham's daughter Frances identified thalidomide as the culprit in infant malformations. (She is honoured in Frances Kelsey Secondary School in Mill Bay.)

For many years, visitors to Duncan contended that they could identify the likes of Oldham and the younger Livingstone as Longstockings by their

Top: Ashdown Henry Green, c. 1874. CVM 998.07.1.2

Right: Lush gardens and manicured lawns were the backdrop for Ashdown Green's Duncan estate, Kilninta, c. 1900. BCARS 75863

speech. "The little town with the accent all its own" was how one visitor described the local tongue. The claim may have been exaggerated, but there certainly was a distinctly British flavour to local usage. A garbage can was called a "receptacle"; should not became "shan't"; "frightfully" was a complimentary adjective, as in, "Shan't we use the receptacle in the play; it would be frightfully funny, you know."

Harold Fairfax Prevost, a McKinstry Road resident, spoke in such a manner. Prevost was the owner of a stationery store and later town mayor (1929–35). His ancestors had distinguished themselves in the siege of Quebec under General Wolfe and on the British side during the American Revolution. One forebear became Governor General and commander in chief of the Canadian military in 1811 and another was a power broker in the USA before dying prematurely (his widow became the wife of Aaron Burr, vice-president of the USA under Jefferson). On the west coast, the Prevosts had been a presence since the 1850s, when the Royal Navy's Captain (later Admiral) James Charles Prevost was stationed in the area. It was in James Prevost's memory that Mt. Prevost (as well as Prevost Island, Harbour and Passage) was named. No other Longstocking family could claim such honours.

Fairfax Prevost's father James (son of the admiral) disgraced the family by stealing money from the office of the BC Supreme Court, where he worked, but Fairfax spent a lifetime dutifully retrieving the name. Blessed with the bland-featured good looks of many male models and a top education at Victoria's Eton-like Corrig College, he was a steadfast merchant, first renting retail space, then buying his own building. Like many Longstocking offspring, too, he was imbued with a sense of public service. He served as alderman and mayor and was re-elected six times. He did not always enjoy the work, but duty was a word that resonated deeply in Longstocking homes.

A respected merchant, local politician and a fine cricketer, Harold Fairfax Prevost recovered the family name after his father had disgraced it. When he was sixty, Fairfax Prevost built his own dugout and paddled it the length of the Cowichan River. CVM 981.03.2.6

In Duncan's Boy Scout circles, Colonel Maxwell Edward Dopping-Hepenstal—CBE, DSO, croix de guerre, 1st Gurkha Rifles—was a living legend. A compact little warrior with nut-brown skin and a habit of speaking in italics, he settled on Stamps Road at Quamichan Lake in the 1920s and remained in the valley until his death in the 1960s. Dopping-Hepenstal had the kind of resumé that awed the most distinguished fellow Longstockings. He

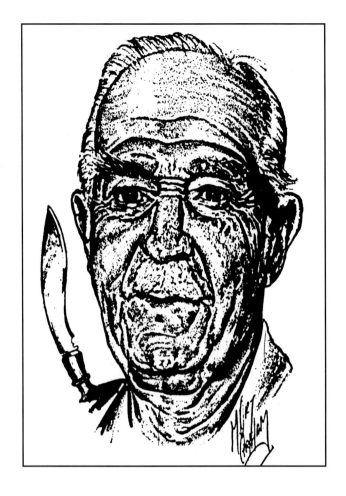

Colonel Maxwell Edward Dopping-Hepenstal in a drawing by Mort Graham, 1954.

was educated at the Royal Military College, Sandhurst—where he played with a witty lad named Winston Churchill—then went on to serve in Aden, India, China and Burma before fighting in France and Mesopotamia. He was wounded in 1915, 1916 and 1917—the last time while pulling his men from a blazing French farmhouse. The event, which left him with a melted-wax scar on the side of his face, was one of many adventures he recounted in his later years.

Much of his career was spent in India. When King George V came to India to be crowned emperor, Dopping-Hepenstal was assigned to help organize a tiger hunt. Six hundred and fifty elephants—the most ever collected in the world—were brought in as pack animals. Dopping-Hepenstal was also charged with setting up the royal camps, which included an exact replica of the king's bedroom in Buckingham Palace and a bathroom with running water so the royal ablutions would not be disturbed. All this he did with the help of tribesmen who could not count and who had never seen a mirror. King George killed twenty-one tigers in ten days. The hunt was so successful that the host, the Maharajah, was heard to say, "I think we've got enough tigers now. There may be another king."

At sixty, Dopping-Hepenstal volunteered to head a leaderless band of Boy Scouts, and was soon promoted to district commissioner of all valley troops. The boys liked him. Heppy, as he was called behind his arched back, was used to leading. For two decades, Duncan-area Boy Scouts followed the colonel's wiry brown legs on hikes over nearby mountains. At seventy, the man was inexhaustible. When the boys complained, he picked up the pace and quipped, "Oh *shut up*, you chaps."

Dopping-Hepenstal's tireless enthusiasm for life was shared by many Longstockings. Arthur Broome's passion was dollhouses. The retired colonel was so set on accuracy he created models with working plumbing. For tiger skin rugs he used the painted pelts of mice. Major F.L. MacFarlane was keen on homemade beer. One of the area's most beloved Longstockings, he delighted in telling Duncanites during the 1920s and 1930s (when he was in his eighties

The Stain of Scandal

A respected civic leader drags his wife onto the front lawn of their Duncan home and pummels her with feet and fists. When she finally stumbles into the kitchen he berates her for having allowed the coffee to cool. The wife of a local butcher and a married hardware store manager arrange for an adulterous tryst in Maple Bay. Their boat overturns and both drown. The son of the local undertaker is discovered to be a necrophiliac. A prominent local doctor is accused of brutally assaulting a boy and leaves for overseas. The seventeen-year-old daughter of a Japanese couple has an affair with a *hakujin* car salesman. She dies of blood poisoning from a backroom abortion and he is charged with manslaughter.

In frequency and species, there is probably no difference between the tragedies that have periodically stained Duncan's social life and those of other communities. Often unpublished, the details of these improprieties have endured in a no man's land between gossip and social history. Yet it is possible to argue that when they did become public, Duncan's tragedies were treated differently than those of other communities. Out-of-town newspaper reports of the unhappiest events were often tainted with smugness, as if the authors enjoyed debunking the Duncan's cut-above image by detailing the rude privacy of its scandals.

A hint of such an attitude is evident in the reports of the mysterious suicide, in 1899, of W.H. Lomas, BC's first Indian Agent, prominent Duncan's citizen, father of six.

A sturdy figure with a handsomely receding hairline, fifty-nine-year-old Lomas was one of Duncan's most public-minded citizens. He was active in St. Peter's Church and the Cowichan Fall Fair. He was interested in his job and spoke Chinook and Hul'qumi'num.

As the article in the *Daily Colonist* following Lomas's death makes clear, his tenure as Indian Agent was not without controversy. It mentions that Reverend Mr. Tait tried to have him

Indian Agent William Henry Lomas. CVM 998.07.1.5

charged—though the paper is thin on specifics. It also says Lomas was reported to be unhappy with his job and was in financial trouble.

But what made Lomas's tragedy so extraordinary was the proximate suicide of a close friend hours before.

At 6:30 in the evening, Joseph McDonald of the registry office in Kamloops told his wife he was going to lie down for a moment. He went into the bedroom and shot himself in the head with a revolver. Fourteen hours later, Lomas killed himself in the same way. The two had been close friends during the 1890s, when McDonald lived in Duncan's.

According to the *Colonist*, Lomas was "in the best of spirits" when he arrived at his Duncan office at 7:00 a.m. in late October 1899. He greeted his Native assistant and asked him to fetch several constables. When the constables arrived they spotted Lomas peeking from a side door. Moments later there was a gunshot.

"Who are you shooting?" one of the constables called out jocularly. When Lomas didn't answer they went into his office. Lomas was sitting in his chair. A revolver was clutched in his right hand. A bullet had entered his head at the back of his right ear. There was a bulge over one eye, apparently where the bullet had stopped.

An on-the-spot inquiry found no evidence of wrongdoing in the case. The newspaper quoted Lomas's son as saying his father had been worried about losing his position. No connection between the two suicides was ever made, and only one piece of evidence with any bearing on the case was discovered. It was a piece of paper on Lomas's desk, inscribed with a quote from the British author George Eliot: "What do we live for, if not to make life less difficult to each other."

---

and nineties) that he was the oldest junior officer on the British army lists. MacFarlane brewed and guzzled his own lagers in such quantities that for four decades teetotallers claimed woefully that he was drinking himself into an early grave. At age eighty MacFarlane took up cycling and survived a high-speed crash on a local hill when his brakes failed. A more militant personality was Colonel Irton Eardley-Wilmot, who headed a sect with views in harmony with those of many Longstockings. The British Israelites believed that historians had it all wrong: the British, not the Jews, were God's chosen people.

Just as the Longstockings affected Duncan, Duncan affected the Longstockings. A few years "in the bush" had a democratizing effect on all but the most stalwart British emigrants. Some actually began to call themselves

Canadians, as opposed to British Columbians. Others went into what their counterparts in England would have sneeringly termed "trade." For many years Commander John Lawrence (Royal Navy, retired), friend of the Duke of Edinburgh, was manager of the local Eaton's. Colonel Ross Smith opened the Silver Bridge Inn and Commander Guy Stanley Windeyer, RN, ran a market garden on the Somenos flats.

Such a change in attitude explains why Bessie Maitland-Dougall was welcomed into Duncan's early Longstocking society. Born to a moneyed Georgia cotton broker, she moved to Duncan after marrying Frederick Maitland-Dougall, a local developer. Bessie was a cherubic brunette who had all the charm and social grace of a southern belle. It did not hurt, either, that her brother-in-law was the local magistrate, or that her husband was descended from Frederick Sears Maitland, the commander of the British warship *Bellerophon*, which took Napoleon captive after Waterloo. In status-conscious Duncan, such credentials opened doors.

Soon after arriving in the valley in 1886, Maitland-Dougall started a local chapter of the Order of the King's Daughters and Sons—the first in Canada. The organization had been founded in the United States by the wife of a Methodist clergyman who wanted to create a non-secular religious order that would do good in God's name. It was intended to give women—and later, men—a vehicle for combatting the evils of industrialization threatening social order: prostitution, slums, contaminated drinking water, poor public health. The movement spread rapidly; by the turn of the century King's Daughters chapters, or "circles," as they were called, were reciting the group's motto in cities across North America: "Look up and not down, Look forward and not back, Look out and not in, And lend a hand."

There were any number of projects that a group of intelligent, socially advantaged women could tackle on turn-of-the-century Vancouver Island. One of the Duncan's circle's first efforts was to help build a Protestant orphanage in Victoria. But Bessie Maitland-Dougall wanted the project to be of benefit closer to home and suggested monies be raised to build "a rest home for tired women, a refuge in time of trouble." A priority was acquiring land. Among those Maitland-Dougall went to see was Angus McKinnon, whose farm bordered Somenos Lake and included the bluff at the northern end of town. Her arguments persuaded McKinnon to donate land with a hilltop panorama of the city and valley. To complete the project, Maitland-Dougall and the committee

Bessie Maitland-Dougall's dream of a home for "tired women" was incarnated as the King's Daughters Hospital, c. 1911. CVM 998.9.2.2

decided they needed $5,000. A Victoria circle seeded the fund with a donation of $500. Garden parties raised more money. When members learned that if they built an emergency hospital they would receive a $1,000 government grant, the convalescent home was astutely changed to a hospital. The project was well on its way to completion when Bessie Maitland-Dougall died while travelling in the USA. The project continued, spurred in part by the memory of its founder, and the King's Daughters Hospital—Duncan's first—was opened in 1911.

The King's Daughters Hospital is often cited (along with grand residential architecture such as The Grange or Ashdown Henry Green's home) as a Longstocking legacy in Duncan. The lasting importance of the Longstockings, though, is less tangible. They brought to the new town a dignity, a reputation it would not otherwise have acquired. These qualities were recognized by Rudyard Kipling, author of *The Jungle Book*, when he toured BC in the early 1900s. Told the story about the Englishman who perished for lack of a cup, he responded: "Every new country needs—vitally needs—one half of one percent of its population trained to die of thirst rather than drink out of their hands."

A nurses' training program was run in conjunction with the King's Daughters Hospital. Pictured above are (front) Miss Nott, Winona Orr, Winnifred Lee; (back) Miss Rogers, Miss New, Edna Murton. CVM 989.1.1.2

4

A City

TURN-OF-THE-CENTURY DUNCAN was an inglorious collection of buildings plunked onto a stump ranch. Chickens wandered the streets and cows interrupted dances at the Agricultural Hall. So many stray dogs prowled the town that men went shopping with 30-30s slung over their shoulders in case the chance arose to get off a good shot. Kids rode pigs bareback down Craig Street. Behind the tudor walls of the Tzouhalem Hotel was, quite literally, Canadian bush. A languid rural air hung over the town, as heavy and indissoluble as the smoke from the valley's never-ending stump fires.

The horse-scented stalls of Keast's Livery, on Station Street, doubled as a gymnasium for the area's yokels, who donned boxing gloves and duked out their youthful energy, or arm-curled a resident black cannonball. The cannonball was the town's talisman. No one knew where it came from. Some said a

Station Street looking east toward the railway station, 1911. Roads blew dust in summer and turned to mud in winter. CVM 987.05.1.6

Royal Navy ship had long ago lobbed it onto a village of unruly Cowichan Indians on orders from James Douglas himself. Scooped from the mucky flats at Cowichan Bay, it had served first as a memento in front of the Agricultural Hall, then as a curiosity on the steps of James Rutledge's barber shop. One day mischievous children rolled the cannonball away from the steps. They pushed it up Craig Street before tiring. That's how the can-

nonball arrived at Keast's. When the yokels at Keast's weren't building biceps with the cannonball, they placed it on the sidewalk. Covered with a top hat, it made a tempting target for a well-aimed kick from a passerby. While the victim hopped on one foot, the boys ran out with a tape and recorded the ball's movement. The record was set by one Al Sutton, of Shawnigan Lake, who on a hot summer day booted the cannonball so hard he moved it a measured 22 feet, 7 inches (about 7 metres) and broke two bones in his foot.

By similarly painful increments Duncan's made the political transition from a ward of the mainly rural Municipality of North Cowichan to an independent city: Duncan. The genesis of this movement is obscure, though given the always divergent interests of farm and city folk it is not unreasonable to presume it dated to a day soon after the Jayneses opened their general store, in 1887. Perhaps a dung-booted hayseed wandered in and left a mess on Clara's clean plank floors? Certainly Duncan's merchants were grousing about the municipal government's apparent favouritism of rural constituents in the early years of the century; by 1907 they were indignantly threatening full-blown independence if North Cowichan did not start providing more services.

What were their problems? Dust. Mud. Taxes. Sewage.

For a town that was already boasting of its verdant setting, Duncan in the early 1900s produced a fantastic amount of dust. Pulverized by horse hooves and cartwheels, amended with the feces of dogs, cows, chickens, horses and indiscreet humans, the rich native topsoil swept, in a talc-fine powder, from the

Stages departed from Keast's Livery for Mt. Sicker, c. 1901. Duncan's prospered from the nearby boom town.
CVM 995.11.6.29

unpaved streets and into homes and businesses. It settled on sills and bedsteads of Ingram Street cottages, on countertops and dry goods of the Duncan Emporium and on the frothy glasses of cool Alderlea Hotel beer men sought to slake their thirst on a hot valley day. Fine and grimy, it defied the most fastidious shopkeeper's efforts to keep an establishment gleaming.

That was in summer. In winter, Cowichan rains transformed dust to slurry. The same unappealing ingredients mixed with rainwater in boot-deep pools in town. The largest of these, described by locals as a small lake, formed at the corner of Craig and Station Streets. Passing carts squirted the green-brown liquid onto storefronts and anybody who happened to be nearby. Businesses built walkways, but to no avail. "It was no uncommon thing to get a liberal douching of mud when passing along the old wooden sidewalks," recalled James Greig, stockman at the Somenos Lake sawmill and later city clerk. As a young man, Greig had lived in a tent amid London squalor, then served with the British army in the monsoon-drenched tropics. Yet he had never seen anything like Duncan's streets. On an early trip through town he observed a lady with a child in a baby carriage caught in the spray of a passing horse and wagon: "She was showered all over—face and clothing (baby as well)—with liquid mud…She stopped to wipe the worst of the filth off the baby and herself before proceeding on her way." Settlers could win the land, merchants could triumph over economic downturns, but until North Cowichan drained and cobbled the streets no one was going to beat mud or dust.

There was the feeling, too, that the municipality was not doing all it could to support community services. Ever since the Quamichan Hotel had burned in 1901, the town's merchants had supported the volunteer fire brigade with money and labour. Their first contributions bought buckets. Chris Dobson, a wheelwright, contributed materials and labour to build a four-wheeled wagon; Robert Grassie, a blacksmith, applied the iron on the same generous terms; Keast's kept it in the livery. Many of the same merchants were on the brigade. When the bell was rung for a practice they dropped their ledgers and ran. The wagon was hustled out from its corner in the livery, a ladder placed against the side of a building and a bucketful of water carried up and flung on the shingles. That was it. The brigade's operations weren't sophisticated but they spoke to a commitment. An equivalent commitment, the merchants felt, was lacking in the parent municipality, whose contributions totalled a single length of used firehose bought from Esquimalt.

Duncan residents read a clear message of disparity into the lousy streets and shoddy services. They felt the relationship between town and municipality should be arithmetical. Duncan made substantial contributions to North Cowichan; it should get substantial returns, too. Evidence to the contrary, such as a report that for annual contributions of $3,000 Duncan received but $100 in road work, fuelled their sense of injustice. "Duncan is hardly getting its fair share of the revenue," declared hotelier Frank Price at an early ratepayers meeting. His outrage was shared by many.

For North Cowichan aldermen, however, the situation was more analogous to family than machine. Charged with administering a territory the size of a European principality but with the population of a single big-city tenement, they had to apportion funds by need as well as rights. Duncan could whine all it wanted about paved roads and fire brigades. Many residents in rural North Cowichan didn't have roads to drive on, let alone a fire-wagon, ladder or even wooden bucket to extinguish a blaze.

Duncan's discontent with North Cowichan remained on a low boil during the years 1907–11. The tension could have become perennial, a microscopic version of BC's ongoing grievances with Ottawa, had the winter of 1911–12 not been so wet. Day after day, through November and December, the rains beat a tattoo on shake roofs, rattled downspouts, flooded ditches. As usual, the streets turned to slime. An "unending mud hole" is how one local described the section of Trunk Road that ran through town; "Slough of Despond" was another observer's view. What made the annual debacle unusual, however, was the presence of nearly pure sewage. Overburdened by the growing town's wastes, the unofficial sewage dump poured forth. Through town the fetid slurry oozed, seeping like a Dickensian horror down lanes and streets. It clung to cartwheels and automobile tires, stuck on shoes, defiled everything it touched.

The grotesque scene was too much even for the subdued *Cowichan Leader*, which climbed down from its long-held position atop the political fence and called for action:

> Under cover of night all sorts of abominations are dumped on the hillside just beyond Duncan within a few feet of the road; garbage and contents of house pans are allowed to be deposited apparently without let or hindrance, and why such a state of affairs is allowed to exist is beyond explanation.

By 1910 the configuration of the Duncan's business district was set. The Centennial Heights subdivision was built in the 1960s from forested land, seen on the far right of this photograph. CVM 980.1.2.5

Is there no one in authority who does not realize the danger to the community that may arise…from passing this decomposed garbage which may contain germs of a disease sufficient to cause an epidemic throughout the district?

The rhetoric played to the hand of the merchants who had been lobbying for a municipal split. Outraged by the condition of city streets and with the weight of public opinion behind them, they moved to form a committee that would see the town govern itself. They met in June, roused themselves with speeches, then broke off to take on separate tasks. To MPP W.H. Hayward fell the job of seeing special legislation passed in Victoria that would enable Duncan to leave North Cowichan and re-form itself as a city; Islay Mutter, realtor, was charged with collecting the required 50 percent plus of signatures from eligible voters; Kenneth Duncan, William Duncan's son, negotiated with North Cowichan over the municipal boundaries.

Once set in gear the machine of independence moved swiftly. Victoria made amendments to the relevant legislation. An agreement was extracted

from the municipality to cede some 345 hectares, including the developed and semi-developed areas around the original townsite. Appropriate notices were published in the newspaper. After years of dawdling, the process over the winter of 1912 moved with disarming speed. On March 4, 1912, Letters Patent were issued and 345 hectares were severed from the southern portion of the municipality to become the City of Duncan.

Who had power and who did not in early Duncan? Women could not hold office, nor could Chinese, Natives, Japanese, Sikhs or any other non-Caucasian ethnic group, no matter how long they had been in the country. Renters could not sit on council, nor could a man who owned property valued at less than $1,000. A man might own a city block but if he was twenty years old he was not eligible for office. To even run for office in Duncan, a candidate had to be a white male and a British subject of at least twenty-one years of age and an owner of land in the city of a value of $1,000 or more.

Such rules disenfranchised 80 percent of the town's 1,500 residents. The remainder were subjected to rigorous unwritten standards that winnowed

With businesses clustered along Station and Craig Streets, Ingram Street was mainly residential. Robert and Margaret Grassie's home on Ingram is shown here c. 1910. CVM 995.11.6.7

many more. To garner the support of Duncan's powerful merchants, a man had to appeal to both sides of the town's uniquely bipolar political psyche. On the one hand he had to pass muster with the stiff-upper-lip Longstockings: a bloodline to the old country counted; so did adeptness with shotguns and hunting dogs. On the other hand he had to fit the standards of the pioneer class, who counted among necessary political skills the ability to put a razor edge on a double-bitted axe or stook a field of oats. An electable man also had to be a member of a club or organization. And in early Duncan that meant he was a Mason.

The Masonic Lodge in Duncan was formed in 1899. Many Masons were involved in the Mt. Sicker mines and their decision to build a lodge midway between Victoria and Nanaimo was a factor in transforming Duncan's from a settlement into a town. The roster of early members is a roll call of Duncan area business leaders. Harry Smith was the second Master of the Lodge in

1900; the wheelwright and businessman Chris Dobson was a member; so were Fairfax Prevost and Hugh Savage, publisher of the *Cowichan Leader*. In 1911 the Lodge was so powerful that the Masons, and not the King's Daughters, laid the cornerstone for the hospital. Their lodge on Front Street was one of Duncan's finest buildings. Anyone who aspired to power in Duncan either had to be a Mason or had to be sanctioned by the Masons.

Such men were necessarily few. Discount the drunkards, the disgraced and the ones who stuttered whenever they mounted a campaign platform, and the city was left with one.

Kenneth Forrest Duncan was thirty years old when he was acclaimed the first mayor of Duncan in 1912. Broad-shouldered, doe-eyed, reticent (and a Mason), he was easiest to define by what he wasn't: noisy, brash, volatile, extroverted. After a lifetime in the valley, people still didn't know what to say about him. "He was no man to sit on a board and do nothing," offered the *Leader*, years later. Some people thought he was slow-witted. A more generous interpretation was that he was self-contained: comfortable in a crowd, competent in business but happiest on his father's farmland, walking with his beloved Irish setter, Rusty.

To this small-town realtor and his band of aldermen fell the Herculean job of organizing the town's political affairs. Their first task was finding a place to

Top: Kenneth Forrest Duncan. CVM 981.3.2.1

Left: Kenneth Duncan's stately home, Brae Head, overlooked the orchard and fields of his parents' farm. CVM 989.10.2.6

The son of William Duncan—and the city's first mayor—Kenneth Duncan (blindfolded) at a garden party at Holmesdale, c. 1912. CVM 989.10.2.7

meet. Cap in hand, the aldermen filed in front of North Cowichan council to ask if they could use the municipality's chambers until their own space could be secured. Then came the bylaws and enabling legislation—the mechanism by which they could govern. Meanwhile, each alderman, infected with the let's-get-going vitality of the newly elected everywhere, had grand ideas. Among the spectacularly impossible ones: a quarter-million-dollar sewage system and an overhead railway bridge. Kenneth Duncan's contribution to unachievable notions was the transformation of the city into a deep-sea port. Dredged from Cowichan Bay to Somenos Lake, a channel would give the little town a doorway to London, Melbourne, Constantinople. Like the other grand ideas, it expired on the planning table. Thankfully, perhaps, the regular business of a newborn town overtook them. The city purchased a former residence at the corner of Front and Ingram Streets. Remodelled, this became the city hall, police and fire departments, police court and cells.

Then began the task of improving roads. Station Street was the first to be "macadamized" with rock and tar. Improvements to other throughways followed as budget allowed. Council also offered to share the costs of building concrete sidewalks with interested merchants. Telephone and power appeared in Duncan with council's blessings. The telephone exchange, operated since 1904 from the Castley house at the corner of Craig and Ingram Streets, was moved in 1912 into its own building at Craig and Kenneth Streets. From an original core of eight subscribers it expanded to include customers as far away as Lake Cowichan. The city's power grid, also born in 1912, boasted twenty-eight electric light customers and thirty street lights. The plant shut down at midnight unless an interested party agreed to pay the $5 per hour extra fee. Then it ran until 2:00 a.m.

ARRIVAL OF FATHER CHRISTMAS.

Incorporation was paralleled by a construction boom the mayor and aldermen endorsed: Cowichan Merchants' three-storey silica brick department store built to replace the one burned in 1911; the ornate Masonic Temple on Front Street; Corfield's imposing Duncan Garage on Duncan Street; a new train station; the urbane Sutton Block on Station Street; the post office on Kenneth Street; and the new school building on Nagle Street.

Muddy streets greeted Father Christmas outside Cowichan Merchants in pre-World War I Duncan. BCARS G-03431

Of these, the post office and the school were most significant, doing for the town what fine china does for a humble meal. Duncan Elementary, as the

The automobile, the central heater and women's franchise signalled Duncan's entry into the modern era. Duncan Garage's wrecker was driven by Ed Fox, pictured here c. 1927.
CVM 990.06.2.6

school came to be called, was created as an accidental consequence of incorporation. When the city was formed, the school district's classification changed from a rural municipality to city status. Members of the board were shocked to discover they now assumed full responsibility for all future school property and buildings. Fortunately the Provincial Ministry of Education realized this was an impossible undertaking for a small town and offered Duncan a break in the form of a 50-percent grant, to a maximum of $15,000. The board recognized a good deal and placed School By-Law No. 1 before the electors, hoping to borrow the maximum.

The bylaw passed in the summer of 1912 and in September the board met to select a site. They had to choose between Duncan's early Alderlea Public School, built in 1891 on Station Street, or a site on Nagle Street next to the recently completed high school. As the latter was in a developing middle-class area, it won out. The school board then sought an architect—a seemingly reckless abandonment of the economical services offered by the government's in-house designers. The man they chose was no designer of faceless educational facilities but one of the most celebrated architects of his day.

William Tuff Whiteway was at the pinnacle of his career in 1912. After living in Newfoundland and San Diego, he had come north to catch the building boom in BC. His list of accomplishments included some Vancouver landmarks: the classically inspired Chinese Times Building and the wedding-cake Pennsylvania Hotel. Undoubtedly his best-known work was the Sun Tower, a stone and steel edifice at Pender and Beatty in Vancouver that held a brief record as the tallest building in the British Empire.

Odd and obsessive, Whiteway was the type of architect who had to be involved in all aspects of a project. In Vancouver he walked the iron girders daily, stewing over the workmanship. It was said he watched every rivet and pound of concrete that went into his buildings. He brought a similar intensity to the Duncan project. One of his first public appearances was at a school board meeting of March 12, 1913 in order to discuss tenders. All the credible submissions were in excess of $30,000. Another architect might have altered his building plans to cut costs. Not Whiteway. With a wave of his suited arm he dismissed any idea of compromise. The board sided with Whiteway and took the alternative route of leaving the four second-storey classrooms unfinished. The two lowest bidders were allowed to resubmit amended tenders. The Island Building Co. won with a bid of $23,930.

Through the summer of 1913, the sound of saw and chisel echoed through the semi-rural streets of Buena Vista. With gantry and block and tackle, workers muscled the structure's massive granite blocks and heavy timbers into place. What emerged was a building so solid and powerful-looking it rendered the newly built wooden high school insignificant. Whereas the high school reflected some antiseptic vision of education as factory, the new building celebrated learning as the highest endeavour. Georgian revival in form and decoration, it featured massive stone stairways and high rounded windows. It carried on its peaked roof a polygonal cupola supported by a massive wooden modillion cornice. The structure embodied many of the aspirations of the day: the British heritage of the settlers, the Imperialist sentiments of the era, the principles of balance, proportion, symmetry and order, which were guiding lights of education.

Downtown, at the corner of Craig and Kenneth Streets, another landmark was under construction. Properly called the Duncan Public Building but commonly known as the Post Office, the structure was going up on the former site of Harry Smith's home. Designed by government architects, the brick structure

William Tuff Whiteway's imposing Duncan Public School (right) was built on the former Holmesdale estate. The Duncan High School (left), c. 1930, burned in 1946. CVM 993.06.9.1

was "commercial Italianate" in style, featuring contrasting brick and stone with an intriguingly broken roofline. It was dominated by a high clock tower which rose twenty-three metres above the unremarkable wood buildings around it. The crowning event in its construction was the installation of clock and bell, both made by the venerable firm of Smith's, in Derry, England. The parts arrived separately, as a report said, "each one clearly labelled, so a boy would have been able to supervise their assemblage." The dials of the clock were 2 metres in diameter, moved by a pendulum that weighed 42 kilograms. To this was added a bell weighing 400 kilograms which required ten strong men using block and tackle to haul it into place. Even so, the stairway nearly collapsed.

The clock on the new building was dedicated New Year's Eve, 1914. Mrs. Hayward, wife of MLA W.H. Hayward, cut a ribbon holding the pendulum. As the bell boomed in 1915, Mrs. Smythe, the wife of Alderman O.T. Smythe, threw a glass of champagne into the maw of the bell. There was something fitting in the new structure, as there was in the public school building to the west,

Duncan Post Office (and later City Hall), c. 1963. The bell, which weighs 400 kilograms, required ten men to haul it into place using pulleys and tackle.
CVM 987.10.1.50

for the residents would set their watches to a timepiece made in Britain. The observant soon noted that the clock functioned as a barometer, too. Whenever the hands were a minute slow or fast, a change in the weather was bound to be approaching, be it fair or foul.

Duncan Neighbourhoods: Pieces of the Whole ⎯⎯⎯⎯

Even before Duncan split away from North Cowichan in 1912, the town's dog-leg configuration was set. Basically there were three neighbourhoods: the Hospital Hill area on the northwest side; downtown or city centre; and the flatland to the east of the railroad, often referred to as the Townsite. A fourth neighbourhood was added in the late 1950s when land on the Cowichan reserve was purchased from the Williams family and the Centennial Heights subdivision was built there.

Created from a section of the former Holmes estate, the Hospital Hill area was Duncan's toniest quarter. James Greig, the long-serving city clerk, lived there; so did baker-cum-mayor James Wragg and the entrepreneurial Hudson family, owners of Hudson's Hardware. In 1911 much of the benchland to the north of the hospital was subdivided and sold as Buena Vista Heights—touted by realtors Mutter & Duncan as being "splendidly situated on high ground overlooking and commanding a magnificent view of Somenos Lake." Many of these big lots were themselves subdivided later and the large homes became interspersed with smaller bungalows.

What little high ground there was in the city centre was built on by the Duncan family: first William Chalmers, then son Kenneth, whose splendid manorial home was at the corner of what became Brae Road and Coronation Avenue. That left the low-lying areas for development. In the beginning, Kenneth and Ingram Streets were a mix of business and residential buildings. As the town grew, the homes were turned into shops, the conversion often as simple as adding a false front to a building. In 1905 James Evans sold approximately 12 hectares of land on the west side of the E&N Railway. This became First, Second and Third Streets—an area of working class homes later settled by Chinese and Japanese families. In 1910, the Duncan heirs sold the east side of their holdings. What was once William Duncan's orchard became First, Second and Third Avenues (later Ypres, Festubert and St. Julian Streets). The area continued to build up until the two Duncan family

A block east from the railroad tracks and Trunk Road was a quiet, tree-lined country track, pictured here c. 1900.
CVM 994.04.5.1

homes remained on small lots. William and Sarah Duncan's house was dismantled in 1939. Some of the salvaged lumber went into a Howard Avenue building. Kenneth Duncan's home survived until the early 1970s. It was destroyed and replaced with a three-storey stucco apartment.

From the 1910s to the 1950s, the area east of York Road was considered the new part of Duncan. Built on the original Lomas estate, the Townsite, as it was called, was a mix of fine older homes and quick-to-build working-class dwellings. Many of the latter were constructed by the lumberman Mayo Singh to house his employees in the 1920s and 1930s. The Townsite was also home to the Duncan Lawn Tennis Club, whose carpet-fine grounds were off what later became Campbell Place.

The club was a social centre until after the Second World War when the club folded and the site was sold for development. Proceeds from the sale were used to build the public tennis courts on James Street, opposite the newly built Cowichan Senior Secondary and to help refurbish the South Cowichan Lawn Tennis Club in Cowichan Bay. The post-war years also saw a restrictive covenant lifted on many Townsite homes. The covenant, dating to the 1920s, prohibited ownership by Asians.

Centennial Heights was Duncan's planned neighbourhood. The 158-lot subdivision was built on 18 hectares of land bought in 1957 by the City of Duncan from the Williams family for $70,000. Brush and timber were transformed into a model of contemporary urban planning. Where they threatened to block views, power and telephone lines were placed underground. Three small parks were interspersed among the development's winding roads, which were named after trees. The acquisition increased the area in the City of Duncan to one square mile.

The Duncan Lawn Tennis Club, pictured here in the 1930s, was on the southern border of the area known as the Townsite. The grounds were sold after World War II, and the proceeds used to build tennis courts on James Street across from Cowichan Senior Secondary School.
CVM N998.11.2.5

A War

BRITAIN'S DECLARATION OF WAR against Germany in early August 1914 altered life in Duncan more fundamentally and swiftly than any event before or since. Overnight, the pervading mood of civic introspection—over schools and waterworks and soiled streets—was transformed into a sense of united purpose. The Mother Country was in need. Duncan must do its part. The city, formally just two and a half years old, may well have declared war on mighty Germany.

Duncan's attention on the war overseas was interrupted only by the great snowfall of 1916. BCARS NA-39825

Duncan's role in the Great War is legendary, cited in Canadian history texts as an example of the nation's strong British ties. The day after war was declared, 147 residents had signed up for the reserve. An entire graduating class of nearby Quamichan Lake School enlisted. So did 58 of the 60-member Cowichan Cricket Club. Twenty-seven men from the 33-man Duncan

Volunteer Fire Department joined. Enlistment ran at an astonishing two hundred per thousand, more than twice the BC average and four times that of Ontario towns. Such figures led to the claim that Duncan contributed more soldiers, per capita, to the war effort than any other community in Canada. So swift and great was the departure of volunteers from the area that by December 1915 the *Leader* was reporting, "Practically all our men have gone." Twelve months later the recruiter in Duncan, a crusty British army veteran named James Alfred Owen, gazed around his office at the empty benches. He signed himself up and left.

Such patriotism was in part a measure of the Englishness of the area. Summoned by Clive Phillipps-Wolley's "voice" of Empire, the Longstockings and their sons and many daughters marched off to do their duty, taking time only to ensure their beloved hunting dogs were placed in good care. The old writer himself tried to join; he was unsuccessful, but his son was commissioned into the Royal Navy. Both sons of James Maitland-Dougall, the local magistrate and government agent, enlisted. William McKinstry and Hamish Kinnear

Members of the military reserve march through Duncan, c. 1915. Reports of the recently departed, of the injured and dead and of returned soldiers was rarely out of the news.
CVM 988.02.1.11

*The 88th Battalion marches through wintery Duncan streets, 1916.
CVM 988.2.1.5b*

Maitland-Dougall, both underage, were said to be so keen to serve that their mother falsified their papers. Hamish went into the army, while Billy chose the navy, a suitable occupation for a family that numbered among its distinguished ancestors a British admiral and a retired commander.

But British patriotism was just one card in the recruiter's deck. There were a hundred other reasons to go. "If ever there was a righteous war, this is one," declared a prominent cleric. News reports of "baby-on-a-bayonet" Hun atrocities filled the papers. It did not hurt, either, that there were rumours of a large German fleet skulking off the coast of BC. The whispered stories existed solely on the basis of that strange wartime logic that posits an enemy's existence on its absence: if the battleships haven't been spotted it must be proof they are lurking close by. A soldier in Europe could strike at the aggressor's heartland.

If all else failed, there was the army's time-worn hook that it offered a chance to travel. However crafty, the lure might appeal to a low-paid Koksilah herdsman who had been looking at the wrong end of a cow for five years. The war, at least, offered a change; a cow's hindquarters would always be the same.

Whether their reasons for enlisting were high- or low-minded, the volunteers looked impressive when decked in army regalia. Waiting at the train station on a chill autumn morning of 1914, the early members of the Canadian Expeditionary Force were clad in smart tunics, polished leather belts and gleaming molasses-black boots. Only a skeptic in the crowd that gathered to see them off would have disbelieved the popular assertion that they would be "home for Christmas."

Few would return.

In a bloodless, second-hand way, the residents of Duncan experienced the war's architecture as did its soldiers overseas: calm, curiosity, shock, a fist in the face, trauma. At first, the war seemed fraught with opportunities for heroism and glamour. Even after the soldiers shipped out (usually by train) there was a sense of adventure. Without men to do the tasks, Duncan women had to learn to cut wood, tend to business, drive a car. There was inconvenience, but also the excitement of a unified effort.

First reports were cheery—as if the war were really like what the propaganda posters promised. Private T. Watson, remembered as a bricklayer on Duncan's principal buildings, wrote home that a bullet had passed through his cap. His greatest complaint about army life was the reek of the trenches, which, he noted, "would kill a coon." "The trenches were quite comfortable," reported Private L.L. Rees, who enlisted from Duncan. "I wasn't half as thrilled as I thought I should be, the only time we were in danger was going in or coming out, that is except from shell-fire, or else trench mortars and hand grenades. Of course," he added as an innocent afterthought, "you are liable to get hurt with those things any time."

Then came the spring of 1915. Overseas, the promised quick assault had mired in mud and the two sides had started trench warfare in earnest. The first reports from the front were disarming in their frank descriptions but reassuring in their tone. Private J.R.M. Ellis, brother of Duncan resident Mrs. Grace Baiss, had already been gassed and seen his comrades "mowed down like grass under a scythe" when he took a stray bullet in 1915. "It went in my left cheek and behind my nose and out by the right cheek," he wrote to his sister. He said he expected to be back at the front soon and signed off with a jaunty "Well, au revoir." Another local volunteer wrote to the *Leader* from hospital in England that he had a "pretty bad time out there" in the trenches. In a single fight his battalion had lost 850 men, including 14 officers. His complaint: he hadn't had his boots off in two weeks.

The *Leader* reported deaths, but it was the letters that conveyed the terrible losses. Scrawled in a trench-weary hand, splattered with mud, they chronicled the deaths of Cowichan boys. It was as if a carload of young men were being killed every week.

"These Are All Duncanites"

Private Lionel Geldhart Marrs was well known to Duncan citizens. He went overseas with the Canadian Expeditionary Force and saw action on the front lines. In 1915 he was hospitalized, suffering from shock. He wrote the following letter from his bed in Ward K-2, No. 5 General Hospital, Leicester, England:

> I arrived here in fairly good trim—just tired, that is all. My nerves are pretty well done in, but don't worry, dear old England is looking after me.
>
> It is really awful to see some of the fearful smashing some of the fellows get. Poor beggars! Their misery and pain must be almost unbearable.
>
> Our last two charges were at Richebourg, near La Bassee, and we lost terribly. There are now left…thirty odd fellows out of 240. Poor Hayward was mortally wounded at Ypres, in the stomach and groin. He was in fearful agony and kept crying out all night, "Shoot me, do please." Young Anketell Jones was hit in the leg but his pal Guilbride…is missing, killed, I think. Ted Southern is dead. Tommy Young, my pal, is also gone.
>
> Jimmy Law, carpenter on new agricultural building who got me out to play pipes that night…was hit by shrapnel in the trench with two others and fearfuly mangled, dying quickly. These are all Duncanites.
>
> Two days before charge at Richebourg four of us were sitting tight in a little dug-out when a shell burst on the top and hit the other three in the head, smothering me with blood, etc. I escaped unhurt except a bad shaking. During the charge another shell knocked me insensible and I remember nothing. Our company was reinforced up to strength [but] when the roll was called there were left 58 in the company of 200. Is it not terrible?
>
> Sergeant Williams, of Fry & Taylor, was shot through the head at Richebourg, gallantly leading the company. Somehow or other I got covered with mud and water and stank like a badger. I must have been a sight. It was probably the mud and water that saved me, the shell going deep into it before exploding.

Everybody in Duncan had some connection to the dead. There was William Burgess, twenty-five, a strapping Scot who was a member of the fire brigade and worked on road crews. He was killed in action in 1915. And there was Fred James Douglas, a harness maker and a gifted athlete whose lofting jumpshots had wowed basketball fans at the Agricultural Hall. He survived the slaughter of the Battle of the Somme, in 1916, only to take a bullet a year later. The extravagantly named Hubert de Burgh Riordan conducted a school of shorthand and typewriting in rooms above the *Leader*. He was shot by a sniper in 1915.

At times death seemed preferable to the horrible wounds of war. E.M.H. Farquharson, son of Mrs. A.F. Smith of Duncan, was shot with an expanding bullet under the chin. He survived—minus his jaw and the side of his face. Private H.C. Bridges, another local, was digging a trench when a bullet struck his entrenching tool and sent shards into his back, leaving him paralyzed from the waist down. Through slaughter and injury, war was decimating the ranks of Duncan's young men.

For those who believed the Empire could do no wrong, there was the terrible realization that war is an egalitarian killer. Privilege did not stop a bullet. The Maitland-Dougalls were a family long associated with British military

Heavy artillery passes through Duncan, c. 1918.
CVM 990.7.23.64

William Macaulay, a Cowichan Leader accountant, was killed overseas in 1915. Cowichan Leader

might. They proudly watched their two sons march off to war, only to see them die the sort of inglorious deaths mass warfare invites. Hamish was vapourized while leading a charge in the hellhole of Vimy Ridge. His brother Billy was sunk at sea by a French airship that mistook his submarine for an enemy craft. Hamish was twenty; William two days short of his twenty-third birthday.

Nor was Clive Phillipps-Wolley, who had thundered so militantly from his fortress at Somenos, immune from the distant war. Soon after joining the Royal Navy, Phillipps-Wolley junior was assigned to HMS *Hogue*. On September 22, 1914, while patrolling the Dutch coast, the *Hogue* was torpedoed by a German submarine. Young Phillipps-Wolley was the first Canadian officer in British forces to be killed in action, a distinction that did little to console his grief-stricken father. The man who the *Toronto Globe & Mail* once called the "loyalist of loyalists" was embittered and disillusioned. "They have killed my only boy...and my oldest friends," he lamented to an admirer. "I who was once a hot favorite for the amateur [boxing] championship (heavy weights) of England, have to stay here and rot slowly....I am sixty-four in years but I am afraid I am an older man really."

Besides the terrible fatalities, there was the sense in Duncan, too, that the men who were going to come home would be forever changed. The optimism that had been written across their young faces could not survive the moral vandalism of the European war. For evidence there were the accounts from the few returned soldiers who cared to speak, and more important, the many whose silence hinted at the horrors they had seen. One had only to read the letters home to realize the boys who had trundled off to war were coming home changed men. "J. has done splendidly," wrote a Cowichan soldier of his brother, also in Europe. "He killed himself 18 Germans the day he was wounded, which beats my poor little total of 7." Another soldier was even more open: "I don't think I ever saw so many dead lying about in all the time I was over there. But now I don't mind. It's just

like seeing dead rats to see dead Huns. I hate the brutes. How I love to help kill them." Such men would become Duncan's leaders, businessmen, fathers.

From the lawn on his estate at Somenos, Mark Green, a local farmer, stood and listened to Duncan's joyous reaction to news of war's end on November 11, 1918. The next morning he wrote in his diary: "Peace declared. Heard guns, whistles and bells going about 2 o'clock this morning. Great celebration in

William and Hamish Maitland-Dougall with their uncle, Fred. Both young men were killed in action in World War I. CVM 987.05.5.1

A mountaintop beacon and a granite cenotaph commemorated Duncan's war dead. The cenotaph, seen here in 1927, in a drawing by Ken Hicks, became a traffic hazard and was moved.

Duncan to-day... The Prohibitionists ought to be hung. Influenza epidemic no matter."

To honour Duncan's legions of dead, the community embarked on a memorial project. Several proposals were tabled: a cairn at the courthouse, a memorial cross in town and a cairn on Mt. Prevost, a TB hospital associated with King's Daughters Hospital. By referendum, residents chose the cairn/cross option. In November 1921, at the intersection of Front and Station Streets, Mrs. J. Maitland-Dougall unveiled the cross, upon whose granite surface are etched the names of her two sons. Eventually a cairn was built atop Mt. Prevost. (Neither memorial remained intact. A traffic hazard by 1947, the cross was hit by a drunk driver who threatened litigation. It was removed to green space near the train station. The cairn remains, though without the beacon, whose light has been repeatedly shot out.)

Then, too, there was the job of reintegrating veterans into post-war life. A Returned Soldiers' Aid Association was formed and the organization staged lectures at the Odd Fellows Hall. There, soldiers hardened at Ypres and Festubert were subjected to redeeming slogans:

Germany tried to end me,
Canada's going to mend me.

and

I went in a fragment,
I came out a man.

"The secret of the cure is in being active," lectured one guest speaker, "thus taking away a great deal of the mental strain. The man who was no slacker at the front will be no slacker at home."

No counselling could soothe the mental and physical anguish of some veterans. Gas victims, in particular, suffered tortuously slow deaths. Harry Parker, the *Cowichan Leader*'s once vigorous linotype operator, was gassed at the front and died of effects in 1919. Private Walter Wilfrid Truesdale, a former partner in the men's furnishing firm of Kibler and Truesdale, signed up in September 1915. He was gassed at the push to the Somme in 1918 and transferred from facility to facility. He died at King's Daughters Hospital on June 20, 1922. Alexander Wallace, a "most promising" young newspaper reporter with the *Leader* in the pre-war years, was wounded in the great advance of 1918. After the war he returned to journalism but found the stuffy air disagreeable. He passed from job to job in Vancouver, Nanaimo, Duncan, then gave up the trade for outdoor work. He died in 1930.

For some the suffering went on much longer. Like a lot of other young men, Fred Fielden had visions of heroism when he signed up with the Canadian Pioneers in early 1916. He was dispatched to France in April of that year but in October contracted blood poisoning and was discharged. Robbed of a chance to distinguish himself, Fielden returned to Cowichan. He took up land in Somenos in the hopes of becoming a farmer. Through the 1920s he struggled. Then came the Depression. Then his house burned to the ground. With each setback, his family noticed, Fielden's mood ebbed lower—a slow sinking his brother attributed to the war.

Near destitute, Fielden moved his family to a rented house on Relingferg Road (Coronation Avenue) in Duncan. He joined the ranks of the unemployed in a futile search for work.

At 11:00 a.m. on September 2, 1930, Fielden told his wife he was going to

H.R.H. PRINCE OF WALES AT DUNCAN. SEPT 26. 1919

the farm to fetch some lumber. On the way across town he stopped at Mr. Phillip's Canada Avenue bicycle and sporting goods shop. Phillip was a congenial man, always eager to talk about guns and hunting. He readily agreed to Fielden's request to see an inexpensive shotgun. He took a 12-gauge hammer gun from the shelf and handed it to Fielden. He then reached under the counter and took from a box three Imperial No. 4 long-range cartridges. He gave the cartridges to Fielden, too.

At his Somenos farm, Fielden ambled past the charred remains of the house, through the long grass, toward the little backyard pumphouse. Cows in neighbouring fields studied him briefly before returning to their grazing. At the pumphouse Fielden leaned the gun against the shack and lit a cigarette. He smoked half, stubbed the remainder, and removed his jacket. He pulled a knife from his pocket and, with shaking hands, tried in vain to cut his own throat. He put the knife down. From another pocket he took a string. He tied the string to his foot and looped the other end around the trigger of the shotgun. Then he put the gun barrel in his mouth and pushed his foot. For Fielden, immortalized nowhere, the Great War had finally come to an end.

NORAH CREINA DENNY

Enclaves I: Queen Margaret's School

OF DUNCAN'S RESIDENTS two things may be said: some are shaped by history, others do the shaping. Most fall into the former category; wars and depressions and prosperity tumble them through life like boulders in a Cowichan River freshet. Even Duncan's celebrated citizens—William Chalmers Duncan, Harry Smith, Clara and William Jaynes—are of this type. They are fine people, whose prominence is largely a function of being in the right place at the right time.

Then there are the shapers, those rare people who divert and direct the flood of history. One of these was Norah Denny. A perpetual motion machine

"I didn't profess to know any-thing about teaching. I never said I did," claimed Norah Creina Denny, seen here in a drawing by Mort Graham, 1955. "But I could always cope with children."

in owl-eye spectacles and sensible brogues, Denny was biologically destined to make a difference. Had she not landed in Duncan after World War I she would have flown with Amelia Earhart or published James Joyce's *Ulysses*. She might have led a country. Instead, Denny co-founded Queen Margaret's School, Duncan's most renowned institution, and imprinted on generations of young women her own unique ideas.

Norah Creina Denny's story reeks of high purpose. Celebrated forebears of her English-Irish family included a Denny who accompanied William the Conqueror to England in 1066 and another, noted by Shakespeare, who tended Henry VIII on his deathbed. Her father was a respected physician. She was educated at the best British boarding schools. During the war she served with distinction as a front-line nurse in France. After demobilization she ventured to Duncan on a working holiday, where she scrubbed floors, tutored wayward students and awaited an opportunity to make something of herself.

That opportunity came late on a January morning in 1921. Denny was hiking from downtown Duncan to her rented College Street cottage when a car pulled alongside. The driver was Mrs. Roberts, daughter of the recently deceased pioneer Mrs. Holmes. Roberts asked Denny if she wanted a lift. On the way up Trunk Road hill, Roberts inquired about Denny's students, then mentioned that her mother's now vacant Buena Vista mansion would make a fine school. The two drove in silence for a moment then Roberts added, "Wouldn't it be a good idea to get Dorothy Geoghegan to join you in having a school, and rent my mother's house?"

That was all Denny needed. Impassioned with the idea, she contacted Geoghegan. The two met over tea in front of Denny's open hearth. They were so ideally suited that, in retrospect, the meeting seems a needless formality in their lifelong partnership. Like Denny, Dorothy Geoghagan was educated and well bred. Her father, a highly regarded Royal Navy surgeon, had retired to the Cowichan Valley where he built the stately Primavera on Westcott Road. Dorothy graduated from Duncan Public School, then attended the University of BC. The university had just opened and was set on establishing the highest standards. On Geoghegan's twenty-first birthday she encountered three three-hour exams (an ordeal she often mentioned to students who complained about a challenging exam schedule). Back in Cowichan she faced the limited job prospects that handcuffed all educated women of the day: teaching or nursing. When Denny called, Geoghegan was unhappily serving as assistant instructor for Miss Young, a somnambulant spinster who arrived at school each day on a dray pulled by a grey mule named Banana.

In the kind of mythologizing that became Denny's trademark, she later related the conversation: "We recounted the difficulties and drawbacks and ever in the dancing flames came the pictures of succeeding generations of children who would come, and who, if it could be the school of our dreams, would go out into the world with the stamp of the school upon them and with its ideals in their hearts." The two made an agreement (Denny would have called it a covenant). Two weeks later they were cutting up sheets for curtains in the old mansion; on March 17, 1921, the *Cowichan Leader* announced, "Miss Denny and Miss Dorothy Geoghegan B.A. beg to announce that they will open on April 4th next a Boarding and Day School for Girls...." They chose the name Queen Margaret's School, after an influential British boarding school Denny had attended.

Like its founders, QMS was different. Where the Duncan Public School offered up a daily smorgasbord of industrial arts and sciences, QMS was a pedagogical boot camp. A boarder didn't go for a term; she went for her youth. The idea was to create an otherworldly enclave where girls learned to be self-reliant, socially accomplished, athletically adept Christian ladies. Forbearance, loyalty, humility and spirituality were paramount themes. "Whatsoever Thy hand findeth to do, do it with Thy might," exhorted Denny during morning prayers. To which the students replied in chorus: "That God in all things may be glorified. Show Thy servants Thy work and their children Thy Glory; and the glorious Majesty of the Lord our God be upon us. Prosper Thou the work of our hands upon us, O prosper Thou our handiwork."

To the logical-minded Geoghegan fell the task of teaching academics: upper level Latin, math, literature. She taught in a plasterboard hat, complete with tassel, and swept from class to class with a breezy nonchalance that suggested dispassionate medieval learning. When budgetary constraints precluded heating oil, she held forth bundled in layers of scarves and wool coats. Students learned Cicero in classes so cold the ink in their wells froze solid.

Denny, however, was more of a CEO for the institution. She instructed younger students and handled school affairs. Both women heartily believed in honouring individual responsibility; in the early years each shook hands with senior students before bidding them goodnight. As well, both believed in discipline. One hated QMS punishment was to spend a day with an apple core slung from the neck—the penalty for littering.

Dorothy Geoghegan handled upper level instruction at QMS—and whatever other chores needed doing. QMS collection

By 1923 increasing enrollment forced QMS from its original quarters. With money borrowed from an overseas connection, the founders bought a 2.4-hectare property that straddled the city border at the corner of the Island Highway (now Government Street) and Gibbins Road. The land had been occupied by a butcher, and bones were strewn throughout. There was a house, barn, chicken coop and a muddy forest and field through which oozed the seepings from upland farms. To the studies of Latin and English literature were added stone picking and stump removal. Denny specialized in the pick, while

Norah Denny: Some Talks and Addresses

"A small grey cruiser lying in dock looking forlorn and desolate, her once trim paint is weather beaten and dingy, guns shrouded in dingy painted canvas covers, her deck soiled with dockyard mud and the feet of many workmen." So began Norah Denny's speech to the crowd of anxious QMS students recovering after the Christmas break of 1927. Denny's speeches were a central part of life at the school, reinforcing the school's founding principles: duty, loyalty, forbearance.

Denny put great weight on the importance of what she called her "talks." On the morning a speech was to be delivered, she practised in the basement of the classroom building, where students in the desks above could hear her voice echoing up the ductwork as she worked on her delivery.

Like many of the classic Greek authors she regularly quoted, Denny relied heavily on metaphor and simile to make her points. Life at QMS was variously compared to a complex machine, a garden, a beautiful view, a grass hockey match, music and a British man-of-war. In the case of the cruiser, Denny folded the image of a ship into one of her enduring themes: without staff and students, QMS was just a lifeless hulk:

> It struck me that [the rejuvenation of a ship] was rather like the beginning of the school year and especially like Q.M.S. because for weeks now there has been hammering and sawing, painting and staining, and everything has been covered with dust and shavings, and no children about, and I thought Q.M.S. was feeling forlorn and forsaken. But now her Staff and children are back and I am sure she can hardly restrain a shiver of joy—she is commissioned. We are still undergoing alterations but very soon we shall all be working in unison. Each member of the school no matter what her position may be is needed to enter all school activities with enthusiasm. Each member must realize that her work, her play, her behaviour is of vital importance to the school. I am going to remind you of some of our special difficulties which we are trying to overcome. Manners: using peoples' names, standing up to speak to Staff, respect to Prefects. Higher Standard of Work: We must strive to raise the standard of our work. We have arranged a system of detention for work that must be done again if poorly done. Christmas exams are going to count for your remove. Then care of School buildings and grounds, and care of books and respect for other people's belongings.
>
> And so if every member of the school does her best to pull together and if we all try to have the kind of spirit which animates the crew of every British ship, there can be no doubt that in the years to come you will be able to look back and feel that you have helped to make the splendid traditions that we mean to have in Q.M.S. and you will have something worth while to hand on to those who come after.

Creating a good grass hockey pitch was difficult in the swamp acreage. In 1935, flood waters covered the school to over a metre. QMS collection

Geoghegan became an expert with the axe. Neither woman let an opportunity for an *ad hoc* lesson pass by. Students recited psalms while they worked, or identified wild birds. "Never use the word 'nice'," Geoghegan lectured generations of students who plucked rocks from the grass hockey pitch. "It doesn't mean anything." Denny used the metaphors implicit in tree removal to deliver stirring spiritual exegeses on tenacity, teamwork, spirituality. "In the work of God there are commonly three stages," she advised, "first the impossible, then the difficult, then the done."

When the grounds were cleared, Denny decided students would benefit from a pool. There was no money to hire workers so they dug it themselves, using garden spades, coal shovels, wheelbarrows. Partway through the excava-

tion, Denny decided the hole was in the wrong spot. With a cheery, "Come on, girls," she set the students digging in another location. When they were fin-ished the excavation, they staged productions of *Ali Baba and the Forty Thieves* to bemused Duncan residents to pay for the concrete. Even so, they could not raise money for a pump and filter. That would have to come later. In the mean-time, Denny added pool scrubbing to the curriculum.

So much of QMS was built on the cheap that parsimony became part of the school tradition. "Denny bums, Denny bums, sitting on a fence, trying to make a dollar out of fifteen cents," was a rallying cry for school teams. QMS students played field hockey with sticks fashioned from arbutus branches. Treatment for a sore throat was not an expensive pharmaceutical but a spoon

By the time the swimming pool was finished there was no money left over for a concrete sidewalk. So the students made do with grass and a wooden boardwalk. QMS collection

The Way Out?

In February 1933, when the Depression was a spiralling series of mill shut-downs and farm closures, the *Cowichan Leader* canvassed sixteen Cowichan men for their ideas on economic recovery. "The Way Out" was an extended series that included the disparate thoughts of an unemployed labourer, school-master, retired civil servant, minister, farmer, financier, lawyer and business-man.

Noting the loss of employment due to mechanization, retired Admiral Rowland Nugent advocated reducing the hours of working men. "I would suggest that all factories using labour-saving machinery should be obliged to work in two shifts; one from 7 a.m. to noon and the other from noon to 5 p.m., no overtime or night shifts to be allowed," he said. "This would allow of double the number of employees being in work…It is no economy in production if by saving labour you have to pay out enormous sums to unemployed workers to keep them from starving."

The solution offered by a poultry farmer named Leonard Fordham Solly was more spiritual than economic: "If the Christian commandment, 'Love thy neighbour as thyself', were followed out more, would not some of our difficul-ties be solved, insomuch that, with the right spirit prevailing, an honest attempt would be made to settle economic problems on a fair and just basis?" he asked.

Neither Nugent's nor Solly's prescriptions went far enough for Mr. Roberts. Like many workers displaced by the economic downturn, Roberts thought the whole economic basis of the country needed to be revisited. The working man has, he said, "sweated for centuries to keep the capitalist class in existence. It is our world; it belongs to us; it does not belong to a few bloated parasitic capitalists. It is only because we are such d—— fools that we work…. Who wants to work but d—— fools and horses?"

Reginald Hodson, the principal of Duncan High School, was also asked for his opinion. "Trade," he said, is "the need of the hour." Making a point that would be as relevant in the year 2000 as it was in the 1930s, Hodson said United States trade policy was a major culprit in Duncan's economic woes. Trade barriers prevented export of lumber and other goods into the USA, yet US goods could easily be found on Duncan store shelves. "For every dollar of goods exported, the United States should be prepared to receive in return a dollar's worth of goods prepared by their customers…Two conditions have to be met before any change for the better in world conditions is to be expected; first, an end to the tariff war and, secondly, a redistribution by some means of the medium by which we weigh commodity values."

of Vaseline. Peanut butter was a mainstay, as was tapioca pudding (called fish eyes and glue). Sometimes Denny's deals backfired, like the time a bargain on local rabbit sent everyone running in the early hours to the bathrooms with food poisoning. Bare-bones meals made treats out of the oddest substances. One black market item was cough medicine: a girl given a spoonful would rush from the dispensary to a waiting gang in the washroom, where she would pass it—mouth to mouth, to the highest bidder.

Everything at QMS was done with a sense of tradition. Soon after acquiring the property, Denny and Geoghegan planted oaks along the drive, then told their students how they had gathered the acorns from Windsor Castle. The drive became Windsor Oak Lane. The dumpy buildings acquired Old Country names such as The Main; school properties were called Innisfree and Capashee. The only warm bathroom on the grounds was called The Black Hole of Calcutta. The pool was Denny's Folly. Even the pets were characters: big King, the bomb-proof horse and Edward, the cat, who had a chair near the dining room door and took mean-spirited swipes at bare knees.

In 1934 Denny decided that a school with a real tradition needed a chapel. The school had a strong Anglican connection and the archdeacon, who had trained as an architect, was delighted to hear of the project. He arrived with a detailed set of plans for an intricate building and proudly laid them out on Denny's desk. After showing off the building's many features, he shyly asked how much she was prepared to spend. "Well," said Denny, blinking behind her glasses, "we have $36." The archdeacon thought he had heard incorrectly and asked her to repeat herself. Then he left in an ecclesiastical huff.

Undaunted, Denny contacted Carlton Stone, a community-minded lumber magnate in the making. He donated the material for the log chapel and the labour to erect it. Nestled under sweeping cedars, the structure spoke to two traditions. Structurally it was pure Cowichan Valley: the walls and rafters were of peeled Douglas fir, the altar arbutus, the pews maple and yellow cedar, the shelves in the vestry white pine, the font a maple burl on a dogwood pedestal and maple base. In detail, though, the chapel was right out of pastoral England. The east side featured a window made of stained glass retrieved during the war from the Cathedral of Arras. Historical knick-knacks lined the sills. At the entrance hung a ship's bell from HMS *Curlew*—a gift courtesy of Admiral Colclough Allen, Denny's cousin.

Even after it was established, QMS never featured the sort of starchy orthodoxy that marked private schools. The school incurred the wrath of conservative anti-labour types during the 1930s when a troup of unemployed men marched through Duncan en route to Victoria. Denny opened the grounds to the protesters and they camped for the night. Instructors, too, seemed to be selected for eccentricity rather than teaching ability. A student at QMS might attend a morning class with Madame M. Orbeliani, a Russian-born aristocrat whose family was chased from the country in the revolution of 1917, then have an afternoon class with Bella Greenwood, a bassoon-voiced athletic teacher and one-time member of Britain's women's grass hockey team. Greenwood once listed her duties:

1. Shingling: the roof over the Head's study had to be reshingled.
2. Interior decorating: cubicle furniture to be repainted every summer, each cubicle having matching colour.
3. Swimming: school outings etc. were often at the sea.
4. Hikes: guide hikes up the mountains, Sicker, Prevost or by rivers.

Morning prayers in the chapel became a part of daily life at QMS. QMS collection

Athletes of the 1930s

No one who saw them run ever forgot their power and grace: the long-legged lope, the etched musculature of their thighs, the hair trailing behind like a scarf flapping in a breeze. Yvonne Dingley, a track and field star, and Olive Gorton, a sprinter, were the most gifted of a remarkable group of athletes that emerged from Duncan in the 1930s. The era saw Anna Kier Patrick twice take the women's singles crown at the Dominion Badminton Championships; local Eric Leney win national honours in doubles; Dick Birch and Noel Radford regularly win Island and provincial badminton tournaments; and the Cowichan Cricket Club power over teams from much larger centres. But it was Dingley and Gorton who won Duncan's affection.

The school's founders sought creative ways to marry classical education with workday duties. In this case students are carting away refuse from a building demolition. QMS collection

Not coincidentally, perhaps, both trained with V. "Bucky" Kennett, a sports enthusiast and later owner of a legendarily

The girl with the "winged feet": track and field star Yvonne Dingley. Cowichan Leader

cluttered sports shop at the corner of Kenneth and Craig Streets. Kennett trained the girls on a grassy paddock on the town's north border that had once belonged to James Evans.

A powerfully built young woman with strong thighs and a slim upper body, Dingley burst into the highly competitive provincial athletic scene in 1934, when she competed in the Canadian Junior Championships at New Westminster. She demolished the fields in the 60-metre hurdles, the high jump, and the baseball throw, setting a new mark in the latter event with a toss of 153 feet, 5 inches (46.75 metres). She would have won the long jump and set another record had she not taken off a metre behind the board. The incredulous judges taped the leap anyway; officially, it was 12 feet (3.65 metres); from takeoff to the mark in the sand was 15 feet, 9 inches (4.8 metres).

For the next four years, Dingley continued to set records and impress crowds with her abilities. At the 1937 trials for the British Empire Games (precursor to the Commonwealth Games), Dingley set a new national record by running 90-yard (82-metre) hurdles in 13.2 seconds. The win earned her a spot on the Canadian team at the British Empire Games in Sydney, Australia, in 1938. She knocked over a hurdle in a heat and was eliminated.

Olive Gorton was more of a hybrid than Dingley. The daughter of Mr. and Mrs. A.E. Gorton, who lived on Alderlea Street, she was a sprinter and nothing but a sprinter. When she cut loose, no one could keep up. Gorton won several titles on the Island but the highlight of her career was a match with the 1932 Los Angeles Olympic Games silver medalist Lillian Palmer. They faced off in the 200-metre run at a track meet in Vancouver in 1934. Palmer got away to a better start, but Gorton crowded her from the 100-metre mark on. The two appeared even at the finish line but the judges determined that Palmer beat Gorton by a slight tenth of a second. Gorton's powerful finish so extended Palmer that the Olympic star fainted. Palmer had won the race, but Gorton was the one left on her feet.

5. Riding: horses from time to time to be fed, groomed and exercised by matron in off duty hours.
6. Hockey
7. Tennis
8. Firefighting: A spark from a fire lit a tree and underbrush on the bank along Gibbins Rd. Matron climbed the tree and eventually put out the fire with dribbles of water from a bucket chain across the playing field.
9. Packing and unpacking boarders' clothes.
10. Skating on Somenos Lake when flats froze.

Bella Greenwood, a long-time staff member (right) instructed generations of students in cricket and grass hockey. QMS collection

Duncan Golf Course ———————————————

Long before the Duncan Mall was built, much of the same area formed part of a sprawling golf links. During the 1920s and 1930s, the Cowichan Golf Club spread over 12.5 hectares of leased Indian Reserve. The course extended from Trunk Road in the north to the Cowichan River in the south and east and west on both sides of the railway tracks. It was lined with bush and the fairways sprouted edible mushrooms which knowledgeable golfers harvested. The clubhouse was a small unobtrusive building with a thick toque of moss on the roof. It was down a lane that ran across from Festubert Street. The course was maintained by an Englishman, Mr. Kennington, from Cowichan Bay.

Each of the Cowichan course's holes was idiosyncratic. A golfer teeing off on the first faced a fairway that paralleled Trunk Road, then buckled in an *L* around a thicket of bush and headed south. The best players drove the ball to the foot of Duncan's Hill, then made a lesser shot to the green. Impatient players tried to drive the ball through the hypotenuse and inevitably spent their first hour thrashing around the dense Indian plum and red berry elder. The second was a long straight drive, possible for local hitters like Ben Colk, who went on to become a professional, or David Crane, whose cracking drives could be heard across town. It finished at a green near the Black Bridge. From the second green, golfers packed their clubs along a trail leading under the Black Bridge to the north-facing third fairway. The secret at the third was to sight the back of the battleship-grey armouries building behind the green and let fly. It was a long drive and the worst that could happen was the ball would bonk off the armouries' plank walls. The fourth fairway was a reverse of the third, taking the golfer back toward the river.

The fifth hole was the most challenging on the course. The tee was built on a jettywork that extended over the river. If it was autumn and the salmon were spawning, their thrashing and fetid smell were a distraction. Ideally, a golfer on the fifth drove the ball over a bend in the river to land at the green; otherwise, the player faced at least two extra shots. Many balls vanished with a plop into the river's swift currents. The sixth hole led toward Strawberry Hill; the seventh brought the golfer back into one of the most challenging greens, the Punch Bowl. The Punch Bowl was a natural depression, which was difficult to find (the flag barely showed above the perimeter) and whose contours confounded the most assiduous putters. From the Punch Bowl the golfer hiked back under the Black Bridge to the eighth tee, which faced east between a corridor of river and bush. The ninth hole led back to the clubhouse and a cup of tea.

Queen Margaret's School would eventually become a front-rank Canadian private school. Its cold-showers-and-classics style of teaching made it a favourite with Longstockings looking for an Empire-friendly boarding school for their daughters. But during the 1920s and 1930s QMS was a work in progress. It was established, but there was an air of energy the founders incorporated into the very curriculum. Alumnae liked to tell a story that summarized those founding years. Not long after leaving QMS, one graduate had gotten into what was euphemistically called "trouble." Told about the wayward girl, Miss Denny refused to believe the story. "Impossible," she said, in her patented conversation-ending tone. "Why, she's a Queen Margaret's girl—and a Guide!"

Known as the Punch Bowl, the seventh green was one of the toughest on the Duncan golf course. It is pictured here in the 1920s. BCARS E-00418

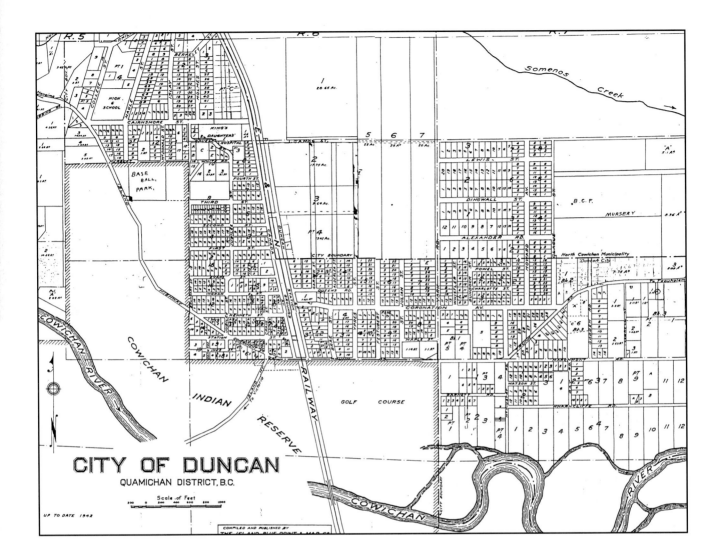

Map of Duncan, 1937. CVM

Enclaves II: Chinatown

FROM THE PIE-SLICE INTERSECTION of Government and Station Streets in the 1920s and 1930s, the view southward extended along a cluttered alley for about half a city block. The alley was walled on the left by the Kong Sang building, run by Quon Kuey Wong. Wong, also known as Jun, was a herbalist and sold roast pig. His rough-timbered building was of the style architects describe as "early Canadian." On the right was a gambrel-roofed structure containing Suey Lee and Sons General Store, landlord Wah Sing Chow's office and confectionery and a Chinese greengrocer. Behind Suey Lee and Sons, halfway down the alley, was a tofu factory tended by an elderly Chinese man who laboured over an immense granite mortar. Beside the tofu factory was a gambling parlour that doled free noodles from a big pot every Saturday. The gambling parlour's far end bordered a stub of Jubilee Street that crossed Government Street and paralleled the herbalist's alley. Jong Chun Jung owned a complex of stores on Jubilee, including a second-hand shop, which Jung ran himself, the Lin Fong

Dragon celebrations, Duncan, c. 1919. CVM 990.08.10.2

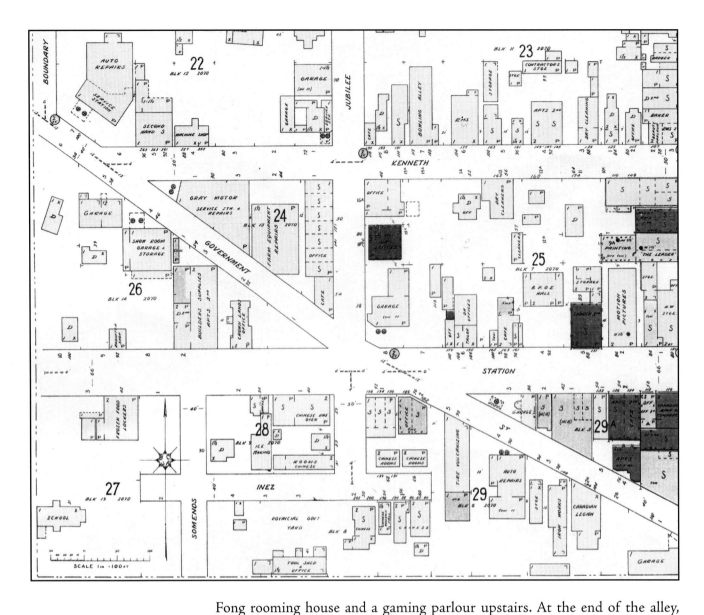

Duncan's southwest corner, including Chinatown, c. 1954. CVM 996.6.4.1 Sheet 2

Fong rooming house and a gaming parlour upstairs. At the end of the alley, between McAdam Street and the Indian reserve, was a hedge-like row of four false-fronted, western-style buildings that housed a gaming parlour, the Sing Lee Restaurant, the Dart Coon Club and a steamy-windowed eatery known as the Pekin. Gracing the front of these establishments were wooden porches and on the porches were wooden benches. On any given weekend from the 1920s to the 1950s, the benches were occupied by legions of Chinese workmen chatting quietly in Cantonese.

Chinatown was incongruous and intriguing. On three sides rose the familiar Duncan—the settlement based on mining, agriculture, logging, Old Country remittances and pensions; the town of Tudor-style bakeries and American-style garages. Yet in one small block there thrived a culture that

Chinese working on the E&N Railway, 1890s. When the railway was finished many labourers took work on local farms. BCARS D-03935

rated a special designation: there was Duncan, there was Chinatown. The rules that applied in one did not always apply in the other. At its peak, Chinatown was the permanent base of approximately thirty Chinese merchants, the centre of activity for the half dozen Chinese families who lived nearby and the weekend destination for hundreds of Chinese miners, millworkers and loggers who had left their families an ocean away to seek prosperity in the new land.

Duncan was still a shack-and-stump settlement when the first Chinese arrived in the early 1890s. Refugees from the CPR building boom, they worked as gandy dancers on the E&N, cut cordwood or became house servants in

Longstocking homes, where their demure manners and padding footsteps reminded their masters of the glory days of the Colonial Empire. The opening of the Mt. Sicker mines brought a flood of Chinese hardrock miners and with them a cadre of merchant-minded countrymen who set up their shingle in the boom town. When the mines closed, many Chinese residents moved from the mountain to the little town in the valley below.

These people saw in Duncan's seemingly steadfast economy the same opportunity that their countrymen had found in the supposedly panned-out sandbars of the Fraser River years before. The Jung family raised pigs in their backyard and sold vegetables. Hip Yick cleared stumps and cut wood. Yuey Wong pushed a modified horse cart about town collecting clothes to be washed at his laundry. From the settlement's economic crevasses they eked out a survival.

Twenty-one-year-old Sue Lem Bing was eager for any work when he arrived in Duncan in 1910. He had a wife in Canton to support and was indebted to a brother for paying the Canadian government's intentionally prohibitive $500 head tax, which was charged on each Chinese emigrant. Bing was a large-boned man with an acorn-shaped head, long, graceful arms and an engaging smile that suggested exactly what he was: an impoverished farm boy overjoyed to be off the fields. In China, he had worked in his father's paddocks and the grimy confines of an uncle's rice mill. Bing claimed he was fifteen years old before he saw his first money. And that was when he catapulted over the handlebars of his bicycle and landed headfirst on the pavement. When he came to, he was staring at a fifty-cent piece.

Bing's first job in Duncan was pulling boards at the Island Lumber Company mill on Somenos Lake. A year later he joined the staff of a local building supply yard. At the time his English was limited to one term: "two-by-four." In 1916 Bing and his brother opened a grocery on Inez Street in Duncan. Bing's Grocery was an unobtrusive building, stocked with the packets of green tea, blankets and linens that were the Chinese Canadian's requisites. Warm and congenial, it became a focal point for the community. In the early 1920s Bing added the Pekin restaurant to the enterprise and Chinatown's geography was confirmed.

By any measure, the Pekin was a Duncan institution. Within moments of leaving the tennis-and-fly-fishing ambience of Staples Store on Craig Street, a person could mount the Pekin's wooden steps and behold a pewful of watchful

Chinese faces. Regular customers who took the time to say hello to these gentlemen might be offered a puff of a hand-rolled cigarette or a sip of tea. Inside, a row of plain wooden tables separated the even plainer booths that lined the walls. At the far end of the room several employees bounced on the end of a long bamboo lever that squeezed noodle dough onto a table. An abacus rode the counter. In the kitchen, fast-speaking cooks dismembered chickens with a single blow of a cleaver. Cats swarmed at their feet and mewed for treats. Waiters slung plates of piping hot food onto tables draped in oilcloth. Above the tables were steam-clouded windows which viewed onto a neighbouring room, where more Chinese men gathered around tables crammed with teacups, towering columns of coins and overflowing ashtrays.

The Island Lumber Company was a major employer for Duncan's Chinese residents. The mill closed in 1916. CVM 993.12.10.1

Overseeing all this was the Pekin's head chef, widely known as Cupcake. Cupcake was tall, with shovelled-back hair and mannequin-hard features. His thunderous voice often rocked the kitchen. When a drunken logger tried to

Sue Lem Bing, 1972.
CVM 991.095.5

barge into Pekin's backroom, Cupcake wielded the cleaver with a dexterity that suggested the next day's special would be woodworker chow mein. If a customer wanted a hard drink with a meal, he asked Cupcake for a Special Tea— Scotch served in a china cup. The Pekin had its own rules, its own constitution. Ian MacInnes, a former patron and local historian, has written about the cafe: "It seemed there was always something happening...or that something was about to happen."

In the 1920s, Sue Lem Bing and Wah Sing Chow emerged as leaders of this intricate community. Both were articulate, intelligent and ambidextrous in the nuances of Occidental and Oriental.

In the parlance of the day, Sue Lem Bing was Duncan's "China Boss." He arranged emigration of workers from China, paid the head tax and transportation, fed and housed them, found them jobs. When Carlton Stone opened an extra shift at his mill, it was to Bing that he turned. Bing received the workers'

Sue Lem Bing's Pekin restaurant, pictured here c. 1969, was a Duncan institution. CVM 987.10.1.11

pay packets and distributed the money. The arrangement led to a lot of mean-spirited speculation about Bing's intentions. If he profited excessively, however, it didn't show in his humble clothing or less-than-glamorous lifestyle. For years he lived in a plain two-storey home on Lewis Street with a picket fence and a cavernous garage that doubled as a temporary accommodation for wayward labourers. The only flourish in his yard was a purple rhododendron. The rest of his small acreage was devoted to growing vegetables to feed his many charges.

If Sue Lem Bing was Chinatown's unofficial minister of employment, Wah Sing Chow was its ambassador. Always well dressed, he had a handsome face and sturdy frame that one observer cheekily said indicated "a good digestion." He was a go-getter, a positive thinker. If, on his way through town, he met seventeen people, he tipped his hat seventeen times. "I've travelled a lot," he said, "both in China and the United States, but I always come back to Duncan—I like the climate and I like the people." He had a lifelong passion for invention and came up with ideas for a cork-lined suitcase that doubled as a lifebelt (which he patented), granular shampoos and a spray-on varnish-like substance to keep paper umbrellas dry in the rain. When Chinatown's tofu maker died, Chow grafted an electric motor onto the former hand-drive and cranked out more tofu than he knew what to do with. A long-held dream of mining diatomaceous earth (used in manufacturing explosives, among other things) from Gabriola Island prospered during World War II.

Wah Sing Chow shared with Norah Denny an illustrious genealogy, only instead of tracing his forefathers to the last millennium, as Denny did, he followed the Chow family line back to the Chou Dynasty of 1072–256 BC. In 1873 Wah Sing Chow's father, Suey Sing Chow, borrowed $200 from a neighbour in his village in the impoverished Sayup area of Kwangtung Province in south China and joined thousands in making the trans-Pacific journey to the United States.

Twelve-year-old Suey Sing Chow smashes the cliché of the classic Confucius-quoting, long-queued nineteenth-century Chinese emigrant. He left his village a committed Presbyterian, sporting a head of curly hair that did not braid well. Both unorthodoxies, the family speculates, may have had something to do with various types of missionary positions held by Americans in China in the 1800s. Jesus Suey, as he was known, worked in California as a cook, laundry assistant, wood gatherer. He raised pigs and chickens and grew vegetables. He preferred mental effort to physical but took whatever job paid. His ambition was to earn enough money to raise a family and eventually retire to China.

Suey Sing Chow. c. 1920.
Chow family collection

At seventeen, Suey Sing Chow returned to China and married. By the time he was ready to return, his US re-entry permit had expired. So he paid the Canadian head tax of $50 and came to BC. He worked for the Butcharts Cement Works in Mill Bay. When the Mt. Sicker mines took off, Suey Sing Chow and Duk Lee, a fellow villager, started the commissary-sized Suey Lee store. The store catered to Chinese labourers. After the mines folded, the partners moved the store to Station Street in Duncan. Between these ventures he returned to his wife several times. He fathered four sons, all of whom shared the name Sing.

PROVINCIAL SCHOOL HOUSE, DUNCANS, B.C.

Wah Sing Chow attended Alderlea Public School. This photograph was taken c. 1906. the building was demolished in 1979. CVM 980.1.2.2

Wah Sing Chow was ten years old when he left his mother and an older brother in China in 1908 and travelled to Duncan. Several years later he celebrated the collapse of China's repressive Ching Dynasty by cutting his braid and getting a fashionable western-style haircut. He was a handsome youth with full lips and strong, searching eyes. He attended Duncan's Alderlea Public School, learned English, excelled. According to his graduating marks, Wah Sing was especially proficient at reading and orthoepy ("the art of uttering words properly"). In his last year at school he was awarded the Good Citizenship medal.

In 1923 Wah Sing Chow married Lai Yee Chow, known to English friends as Helen. Lai Yee was a rare find: less than 8 percent of the Chinese Canadian

population at the time was female. She was the daughter of an aristocratic mother and a fabric merchant. As a schoolgirl in Victoria, Lai Yee once hacked loose the braided hair of a girl seated in front of her. Traditionally, Chinese wore their hair loose only when in mourning; to do otherwise was to invite ill fortune. The rash act humiliated Lai Yee's father and she was pulled from school, thus ending her English education. Lai Yee felt trapped by her halting English for the rest of her life.

Wah Sing and Lai Yee soon became a leading couple in the community. Lai Yee tended their home at 279 Evans Street and raised eight children: sons Edward, Edmond, Edwin and Edgson, and daughters Virginia, Viola, Effie and

Helen Lai Yee Lowe and Wah Sing Chow (second and third from left) were married in May 1923. The Chows had businesses in China and Canada.
Chow family collection

Janie. Wah Sing took over his father's business and changed the name to Suey Lee & Sons, which was eventually incarnated as Chow Brothers Grocery, run by Wah Sing Chow's China-born nephews, Wai Dai (Willie) and Wai Hong (Hank) Chow.

Chow family collection

But commerce was only a fraction of Wah Sing Chow's interest. He and Lai Yee learned western dances and he built furniture and contributed articles to newspapers. His writing reflected his own inspirations, mixing scholarly exegeses on Canadian immigration policy with quotations from Confucius. He was involved with the Rotary Club, the *Chinese Times* newspaper (published in Victoria, Vancouver, Toronto and the USA) and a secretive organization that kept a hall next to the Pekin and was known as the Chinese Freemasons.

The Chinese Freemasons, or Chee Kung Tong, was founded in the 1860s by emigrant gold miners lobbying for the overthrow of China's Qing Dynasty. The dynasty fell in 1911 but the organization endured. When Japan invaded Manchuria, the Freemasons raised money for the war. In the early years, especially, the Freemasons were not without opposition and they adopted a complex set of secret gestures and oaths. One example, cited by Anthony Chan in *Gold Mountain*, was "not to debauch a brother's wife, daughter, or sister: if you do, may you perish under the knife." Members also pledged "not [to] avenge private animosity under the pretext of a public wrong, thus covertly scheming to injure a brother: if you do, may you be bitten by a tiger when you ascend a hill, may you drown when you go into water." If a Freemason wanted to verify that a dinner mate was a fellow member, he placed a chopstick across his outstretched fingers and held out his hand, as if in offering. The correct response was to push a near-by teacup away. In Freemason slang, police were "a current of air," killing was "washing one's ears" and to belong to the Freemasons was "to be born." When the Freemasons were infiltrated by support-ers of the much-reviled Nationalist party, they formed the even more exclusive Dart Coon Club. Wah Sing Chow was a mem-ber of that benevolent organization, too.

In Duncan the Chee Kung Tong and the Dart Coon Club took on the roles of community organizations. The Chee Kung Tong was instrumental in fundrais-ing for an independent Chinese school on Second Street. The Dart Coon Club became a weekend recreation centre, where musicians gathered and formed an impromptu orchestra.

Wah Sing Chow was also a member of the Chinese Consolidated Benevolent Society (CCBA), more commonly called the Chinese Six Companies. This group was so influential that it was called the Supreme Court of North America Chinatowns. The roots of the organization are obscure, but it grew from the need for the Chinese community in California to have a representative to act on their behalf in dealing with the government. In the 1880s, businessmen from Victoria's Chinatown, then the largest in Canada, founded a local chapter of CCBA. They funded it by sending out a province-wide notice asking for every Chinese to donate $2. Included on the notice was a warning that anyone who did not contribute would have to pay $10 before the association would

Chinatown was off-limits to daughters of Duncan's Chinese families. These girls, from the Chow, Lum, Thom and Wang families, were part of the United Church's CGIT (Canadian Girls in Training), 1942. Chow family collection

Duties of the Duncan Police Constable ————————

(taken from police day books for the years 1921 and 1924)

1. Patrol the town.
2. Meet all trains.
3. Direct traffic when required.
4. Investigate auto accidents.
5. Serve summons.
6. Investigate reported robberies.
7. Enforce B.C. Prohibition Act.
8. Check persons supplying liquor to the Indians.
9. Enforce narcotics laws.
10. Appear in Court.
11. Attend prisoners in the jail.
12. Attend house fires.
13. Make fire inspections.
14. Clean, hose and load the fire truck.
15. Sanitary inspections, including cess-pools.
16. Checking on reports of cruelty to farm animals.
17. Destroying sick dogs.
18. Rounding up and impounding stray cattle.
19. Selling unclaimed animals at pound by auction.
20. Reading the electric meters.
21. Collecting business licenses.
22. Collecting dog taxes and road taxes.
23. Collecting poll taxes from Chinese and Japanese.
24. Issuing building permits.
25. Hiring men to cut thistles on vacant lots.
26. Investigating cases of want.
27. Investigating immigrants.
28. Checking for criminals whose descriptions have been circulated.
29. Making monthly reports to Prohibition Commissioner.
30. Storing "found" bicycles.
31. Posting public notices.

allow them to return to China. Since the CCBA's founders were shipping agents, or friends of shipping agents, it was easy to deny steamship passage to anyone who failed to produce a donation receipt. Within a year of registering in BC, the organization had raised $30,000. Soon there was a CCBA chapter in every west coast Chinatown.

It fell to Wah Sing Chow, as the most literate member of Duncan's Chinese community and a local CCBA leader, to be a *de facto* representative in dealings

Drug Bust

Under the blanketing darkness of a stormy February evening, a RCMP cruiser rolled to a stop near the White Bridge, just south of the City of Duncan. Inside, two constables listened as an officer gave final instructions to a plainly dressed informant: walk into Duncan, go up the stairs of the Mei Ming building and purchase narcotics. He was to pay with marked bills and he was to keep any purchase as evidence. As soon as he returned, the police would move in for the arrest.

The events took place on the evening of February 23, 1930. RCMP Sgt. J.R. Paton and two constables had driven from Victoria with O Yung Wai, a Vancouver resident who freelanced as an informer. Wai left the cruiser and walked into Chinatown. Between the Kong Sang Building and Suey Lee's Store he found an alleyway. At the end of the alley, stairs led to a dimly lit hall. In a room off the hall Wai found five men sprawled on mattresses. Two men were smoking opium. Another, later identified as Chow Duk Yuet, was asleep. Wai woke Yuet and asked him to sell $4 worth of opium.

"Four dollars' worth?" asked Yuet, sleepily. Wai said yes. Yuet took four foil-wrapped decks from his trouser pockets and handed them to Wai. Wai gave him the money and left.

Outside, Sgt. Paton glanced at Wai's purchase then signalled his constables to move in. Two policemen stormed the drug dealer's room while another waited outside. Yuet dashed but made it only as far as the chest of a burly cop stationed in the hall. A search of Yuet's trousers revealed several decks of opium, plus the marked money. A fully equipped opium-smoking den was also found in an adjacent room, including pipe stems, bowls, rolling papers, cooking needles and bottles of residue.

Such Chinatown busts were not unusual in Duncan in the 1920s and 1930s. The irony of the town's small-scale opium war was that it was actually the result of nineteenth century British foreign policy. In the early 1800s Britain introduced India-grown opium to China as a way of countering a huge imbalance of trade caused by the tea trade. By mid-century there were ten million opium addicts in China; the drug acquired a status of sorts, as cocaine would later. Opium smoking was one way a Chinese immigrant in Canada could show his success.

Among Duncan's non-Chinese community such drug raids encouraged the opinion that Chinatown's economy had some unsavoury aspects. Because the transactions were most often between Chinese, however, the activity was seen more as a nuisance than a menace. The other common charge was for bootlegging liquor, often to Natives. For Yuet, the historical footnotes of the opium trade were probably meaningless. He was sentenced to six months in jail for selling narcotics.

---

with the town. After the stock market crash of 1929, that role became increasingly difficult. All over BC the Depression pitted Caucasians against Chinese, but in Duncan anti-Asian feelings ran especially high—as if in equal and opposite proportion to the town's Britishy self-image. There were calls for the highest authorities to remove Chinese competition from job markets: "It is not the desire merely to limit the rights of Orientals, but 'to ascertain the practicability of the removal from the country of all Asiatics and the expropriation of all property owned by them'," reported the *Leader* on March 6, 1930. Among the keenest supporters was the Cowichan branch of the Canadian Legion. Cowichan's elected officials also sided with the exclusionists. MLA C.F. Davie proposed an amendment to the Marriage Act that would prohibit marriage between a white person and a person of Chinese or Japanese race and Kenneth Duncan, MP, argued for legislation restricting the rights of Orientals to own or lease farmland.

Wah Sing Chow's response to the sudden chilling in racial relations spoke to his bicultural heritage. At the personal level, he continued to be gracious and generous. Every Christmas he distributed many turkeys to Duncan residents and merchants. Every Christmas the family received many turkeys in return. He hosted dinners for local teachers, doctors and police. He neither looked nor acted like a man besieged by racism.

In his public life, however, Chow was a vigorous defender of Chinese interests. In a lengthy letter-cum-essay to the *Cowichan Leader*, published March 31, 1930, he dissected the arguments of the anti-Asiatic element: how was it, he asked, that Canada could impose a head tax of $50, and later $500, on Chinese immigrants, yet now contemplate banning them from owning land? These were the workers the government had shipped in to build the railway. They had stayed, found work, contributed to the country. They had every right to remain in Canada.

But it was to the mixed marriage motion that Chow made his most emotional objection. He wrote: "It is a most reliable policy to bring the world into peace, free from warfare forever, by advocating the inter-marriages between persons of different countries, irrespective of race whatsoever. By doing this the relationship between all countries in the world may become more closer every day and they betterly understand each other, consequently, a total elimination of warfare might be achieved."

Though Chow took his family to China for business and schooling during the 1930s, he never gave up his calls for racial equality, and he returned to Canada

in 1936 to find anti-Chinese feelings were abating. After the Second World War a number of Duncan's prominent businessmen and other leaders, including Davie, apologized to Chow for their pre-war remarks.

In his own way, Charlie, manager of Charlie's Palace of Pool, smoothed the fabric of race relations in Duncan, too. Charlie's Palace of Pool was below Suey Lee and Sons General Store, in a shadowy hall that remained cool on the hottest August day. The pool hall was where local youths honed their skills before venturing to Ivan's Pool Hall, the shark-ridden cave below the Greenhaven Cafe. Charlie was a mischievous character with two thumbs on one hand which he used to advantage when playing pool. He seemingly lived behind the counter, where he drummed his fingers incessantly on the countertop rubber change mat and brewed herbal concoctions of cabbage and octopus on a hot plate. The only time Charlie emerged from his position behind the

The Vancouver opera singer Helena Wong joined Duncan residents Virginia Chow, Kay Wong, Georgina Thom and Marion Chang for a China Relief fundraiser, c. 1943. Chow family collection

counter was to goose unsuspecting players with the butt end of a cue. It was said you could always spot a local pool player who trained at Charlie's because they hovered over a pool table nervously, legs together, as if something unexpected had just happened, or was about to happen.

Wah Sing Chow's son Edward won first prize for his tank float in 1944.
Chow family collection

Duncan's Chinese community supported China in the war with Japan. This fundraiser was held on Inez Street (later McAdam) in 1944.
Chow family collection

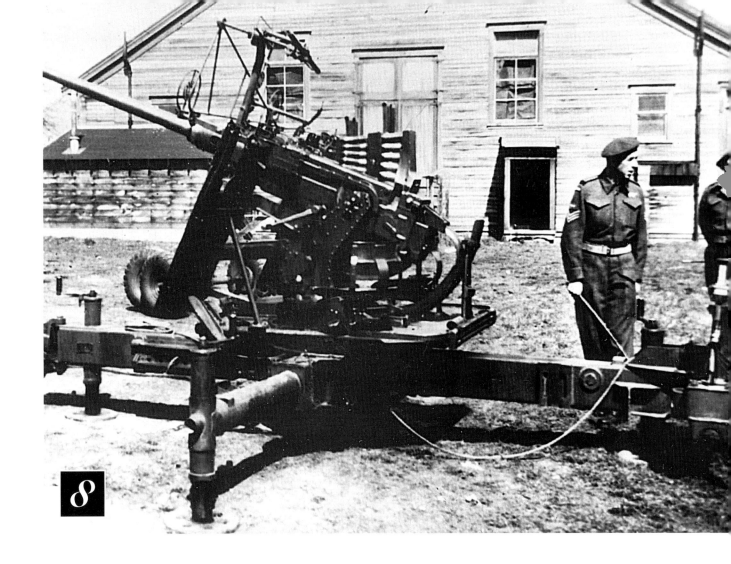

World War II

"WHETHER YOU LIKE IT OR NOT, I am here to tell you that you are going to be bombed this year," declared William Oswald, BC's assistant provincial fire marshal, to an audience of one hundred firefighters and emergency workers at the school gymnasium in Duncan. An explosives expert, Oswald was preparing coastal towns for air strikes and possible invasion. It was winter 1942. Japan had just attacked the US Navy base at Pearl Harbor, Hawaii. Canada's sprawling west coast, largely ignored while the country focussed its efforts on the war in Europe, seemed a likely next target. "The Battle of Britain was fought by the air force and the firemen," Oswald continued. "The Battle of BC is going to be

The installation of an anti-aircraft gun behind the armouries during World War II was a graphic reminder of Duncan's vulnerability to sudden attack.
CVM 996.01.2.5

dealt with by the firemen." He detailed to the astonished crowd the damage that was to be visited on the town: craters 20 metres in diameter blown into Station Street; fragmentation bombs spraying shrapnel at groin level amid crowds at the Agricultural Grounds; fire bombs setting Buena Vista homes ablaze. Devastation, dismemberment, death would be commonplace. According to Oswald, the question was not if the town was going to hurtle into chaos, but when.

The bombs didn't fall, the town was not overrun. But the fear and mistrust that the Pacific war delivered on Duncan were incendiary. War engulfed the town like the autumnal pall of loggers' slash fires. Sand piles appeared at street corners, windows disappeared behind blackout curtains, air raid sirens wailed in spine-chilling rehearsal.

By 1941, Duncan had been involved in the conflict in Europe for two years. In both rate of volunteerism and vigour of support, the town was upholding its First World War legacy. Scores of young men enlisted, many waving so-long from the same E&N carriage windows that had framed a generation of departing volunteers a quarter of a century earlier. At home, families and friends scrimped on fuel and luxuries in aid of the war effort. Housewives swapped cotton frocks for leather aprons and took jobs left vacant by departing soldiers. The Canadian Legion supported Victory Bond drives, the Cowichan Women's Institute organized a boycott of imported mandarin oranges. Such efforts were earnest and well-intentioned. Half a world from the blistered streets of London, Duncan was waging a bombless war.

Then, on December 7, 1941, Japan attacked Pearl Harbor. Canada declared war soon after. Suddenly, Oswald and others were saying Duncan was an *X* on a Japanese aviator's map. The very qualities that made Duncan peaceful—the distance from larger centres, the expanse of surrounding fields and forest— now made it vulnerable. It didn't take a military strategist to conceive a likely sequence: carrier-based planes launch off the west coast; bombs rain thickly; parachutes blossom in the sky; battle-hardened paratroopers secure the Island Highway north and south of town. With only negligible losses to the invading force, Duncan could be sealed off like an occupied Pacific island. As the *Cowichan Leader* put it in January 1942, Duncan was "like the neck of a chicken stuck out waiting for the axe."

Such a scenario was behind the frenzied organization of Duncan's wartime defences. Armed sentries were stationed at the waterworks, and Joe's Tire

CITY OF DUNCAN

AIR-RAID PRECAUTIONS

On the recommendation of the CHIEF WARDEN I wish to draw the attention of all citizens to the following:—

The Protection of Individual Houses and Business Premises Against Incendiary Bombs Is the Duty of the OWNERS and OCCUPIERS of Such Premises

To do this keep a bucket or small sack of dry sand in a convenient place on your premises at all times. Sand may be obtained from dumps which have been made at the following points in the city:—

AT THE INTERSECTIONS OF

McDonald—Cairnsmore	Bundock—Coronation
Holmes—Cairnsmore	McKinstry—Coronation
Berkeley—Holmes	Alderlea—Queens
Boundary—Cavell	Ypres—Queens
White—Jubilee	Powel Street, east end
First—Jubilee	Charlotte—Bundock
Second—Jubilee	Duncan—Trunk
Third—Jubilee	Brae—Trunk
Evans—Jubilee	Ypres—Trunk
Ingram—Jubilee	Festubert—Trunk
Kenneth—Jubilee	St. Julian—Trunk
Inez—Jubilee	York—Trunk
Brae—Coronation	Maple—York
Ypres—Coronation	Campbell's Corner
Festubert—Coronation	Watson—McKinstry
St. Julian—Coronation	Wharncliffe—McKinstry
York—Coronation	Day—Wharncliffe
	Godden—Marchmont

Also on the School Grounds, at the City Hall, and at the City Gravel Pit on Bell-McKinnon Road.

Sand in the wooden boxes on the streets must NOT be removed. It is for use of firemen only.

DO NOT USE CHEMICAL FIRE EXTINGUISHERS ON INCENDIARY BOMBS

MORE VOLUNTEERS ARE REQUIRED FOR WARDEN DUTY IN THE CITY

Men over 16 years of age and unfit for other duties should apply to A. J. Castle, or at the City Hall, or to the warden whose name is on your A.R.P. card.

E. W. LEE, Mayor.

Air raid warnings and blackouts were part of Duncan life following the attack on Pearl Harbor in 1941. The Cowichan Leader *also ran articles on bomb disposal techniques.*
Cowichan Leader

Hospital was designated an emergency first aid station. The Cowichan Rangers were formed. Part of a coast-wide organization set up by the army, the Rangers were to fight a guerrilla-type war in the mountains, the valley and, if necessary, the town. There were several Ranger companies in the valley, each with one hundred men. These men were too old, too young, handicapped or otherwise disqualified from regular service. Duncan was represented by No. 17 Company, headed by Geoffrey Knighton Hobson, a Wilson Avenue veterinarian. Armed with vintage Winchester '98 30-30 rifles, Hobson and his company were to be the first line of defence if an invading force approached Duncan.

Individuals, too, took part in the fortification of homes and businesses. When war was declared on Germany in 1939, Norah Denny put her funny little British car up on blocks. Then she and Dorothy Geoghegan started a scrap drive to aid the war effort. Pound by pound—and over the indignant protests of some moneyed families who did not fancy their daughters sifting metal—QMS students collected cans, foil and junk. In all, they raised $5,000—enough to buy a landing craft. With word of a possible air attack, Denny had students camouflage the school's aquamarine-coloured pool with painted octopus and fish. The two teachers cashed in their life insurance policies and built a concrete air raid shelter under Gibbins Road. Inspected by the military, it was declared the best on Vancouver Island.

Inevitably, the attention of the war-minded came to rest on Duncan's Japanese community. Too small to support a commercial core like Chinatown, this settlement was centred on several Japanese homes and market gardens below Hospital Hill. "Jap Land," as it was known, was an identifiable enclave with a store, a leader and its own distinct, if minuscule, history.

The first Japanese settled in Duncan at the turn of the century. Yoshitaro and Mitoko Asada abandoned jobs at a seedy Victoria hotel in 1903 to become domestics to Cowichan Longstockings. There were so few Japanese in the area that they posted a sign outside their Duncan home inviting any passing Japanese to drop in. The home became a focal point, as did a general store they later opened at the west end of Station Street. Arriving in Duncan around the same time as the Asadas was Mantaro Nagano. A small man with copper-beech skin and a gentle manner, Nagano had left his wife in Japan in the 1880s to find his fortune in North America. He had worked as a coal miner in central Washington and as a packer at a Steveston, BC cannery. In Duncan he purchased a few hectares of rich bottomland around Third Street and sold carrots, potatoes, celery and sweet corn said to be so tasty some families made whole meals of it. Nagano, called Ji-Son (Grandpa), became the spiritual father to this small community.

Eighty to ninety Japanese gathered around this core and found work in the area's mills, started businesses, raised families. The Miyake family opened a store on Station Street (All Kinds of Fish for Sale. All Kinds of Help Supplied); Okazaki was a tailor who also sold Japanese porcelain and curios; the Toyotas had a farm on the flats below the hospital. Many Japanese worked at the sawmills at Hillcrest or Paldi. If the Duncan settlement was never the size of Japanese communities in Chemainus or Paldi, it had its own character. It was more relaxed, less under the thumb of the tradition-minded Issei (first-generation Japanese). Defiant Japanese kids from Chemainus sneaked away to Duncan to learn western dances like the Big Apple, or to feast on greasy cheese-burgers at the Cecil Cafe.

Leaders of Duncan's Japanese community gathered in front of Asada's store in 1919 with the visiting Japanese Consul. Kay Fujiwara

Charles Hoey, VC

Charles Hoey was twenty years old when he left Duncan to join the British Army in 1934. He became a top soldier in the Second World War, cited several times for bravery in battle and posthumously earned the celebrated Victoria Cross. If ever a local boy was destined to be a war hero, it was the lad everyone knew as Charlie.

Clean-cut, with high cheekbones, jug-handle ears and tar-black hair, Charles Ferguson Hoey was the son of a Duncan businessman, Ferguson Hoey, whose father was a decorated British Army officer. Ferguson had forsaken the family's military tradition and, along with his wife Mary, had come to Canada from Britain. They tried raising poultry, then in the 1920s Ferguson joined J.H. Whittome & Co., where he rose from bookkeeper to director. Active members of the Duncan Tennis Club, the Hoeys lived in a stylish but unassuming home at 745 Wharncliffe Road. They had three children. Charlie was the eldest.

From an early age Charlie knew he was destined to be a soldier. He and his brother Trevor (also killed in the war) built a heavily buttressed fort in a sprawling backyard maple and spent many hours rat-atat-tatting fictitious enemy battalions. Charlie also used his lunch hours at Duncan Grammar School, opposite QMS (and later the site of the Cowichan District Hospital), to build an even more elaborate series of ground forts. He excelled at school sports where he played on the school's First XV in rugby and the First IX in cricket. He was also a keen naturalist and boasted an excellent butterfly collection. Whatever Charlie Hoey did, he did well.

After graduation Charlie travelled to England and attended the Royal Military College at Sandhurst, then served with the Lincolnshire Regiment. He was stationed in India when the Second World War broke out.

Many of Charlie Hoey's wartime operations were covert. In 1943 he led forty soldiers behind enemy lines during a night raid at Maungdaw. According to a Duncanite who met them afterward, their booty included mementos of the Japanese soldiers they had killed, such as documents and family photos. The raid earned Hoey a Military Cross.

Charles (left) and Trevor Hoey died fighting in World War II. CVM 994.11.2.2

The firefight in which Charlie Hoey died was one of those skirmishes on which battles and even campaigns turn. In early 1944, the Japanese army halted a British advance in Southeast Asia by taking control of Burma's Arakan Hills. The low camelback range was a textbook defensive fortification, with many ravines in which to embed gun stations. With the British advance deadlocked, Hoey's company was ordered to lead the assault on a key Japanese Army fortification. After days of fighting up a valley bottom that was swathed with gunfire from the surrounding hills, Hoey came up against a well-entrenched machine gun nest, dubbed the Admin Box, which could only be taken by a frontal assault. Hollering "Follow me!" Charlie Hoey sprinted up a stream bed toward the installation, firing a machine gun from his hip. All around him men were gunned down. Charlie was hit in the face and legs but kept on. When his own weapon failed, he grabbed a bren gun from a fallen soldier and kept shooting. He succumbed as the fortification was overrun. The British advance continued. The Canadian hero was buried on the mountain where he died.

As one of only two Canadians awarded the Victoria Cross in the war with Japan, Charlie was written up in newspapers from coast to coast. His posthumous decoration was accepted by Mary Hoey at a ceremony in January 1945. "If there be one lesson that the boys and girls of Cowichan can take from his life and example," declared the *Cowichan Leader* the same week, "it is that while scholarship and brilliancy at lessons are desirable assets, they are not the greatest essentials. Charlie revelled in the outdoors. He had gifts of leadership. He had dogged determination. The battle in Burma was won on the playing fields of Duncan."

Matanabe was one of several Japanese loggers who lived in Duncan. CVM 989.07.1.2

Such an atmosphere appealed to Shigeo and Elizabeth Kato. The young couple moved to Duncan with their two children in 1938. One of only a dozen Japanese British families in all BC, they had met in Vancouver in the mid-1920s. Tony, as he was called away from home, was the son of first-generation immigrants who operated a shingle mill on the North Shore. He had movie star looks and an athlete's body he had often shown to advantage while swimming at Vancouver's popular English Bay. His many admirers included Elizabeth Ellen Crowther, a London-born beauty with an alluring smile and attractive figure. The two met at a beach party, fell in love and eloped to Nanaimo, where they married.

Such an interracial union was anathema for the conservative, tradition-minded parents of both newlyweds. Elizabeth was effectively shunned by her family, and Tony was rebuked by his parents for taking up with a *hakujin* girl. Defiantly, the two struck out and went upcoast, where Tony worked in a logging

camp and Elizabeth bore two children, Robert and Marion. When the Depression closed the camps, the family moved to Duncan to rent a humble house at 727 Marchmont Road. Tony went to work as a high rigger for Mayo Logging. Elizabeth set about creating a standard working-class home in what they both hoped would be a tolerant, non-judgemental community.

The Japanese community suffered one of the most dramatic effects of the war. After repeated calls from Duncan's political and business elite, they were expelled from the coast with some 22,000 other Japanese Canadians—many of them Canadian citizens—and their property was seized and sold. The story of their removal and internment is testimony to the emotions that war, real or imagined, can unleash—emotions that are almost incomprehensible nearly sixty years later.

Tony Kato and
Elizabeth Kato.
Robert Cato collection

Mantaro Nagano grew vegetables in his Third Street garden and delivered them by truck door to door. Sayoko Kawaguchi collection

Perhaps because it was so adamantly pro-British, Duncan's Caucasian community in the 1930s tended to view local Japanese as individually admirable but collectively reprehensible. Even in peacetime this curious form of xenophobia led to some extraordinary incidents. A city alderman might congenially purchase chard, potatoes and carrots from Mantaro Nagano in the afternoon, then that evening holler in council about the "Oriental Menace." A Japanese student might top a competition at the Duncan Public School only to be cited as a local example of a startling province-wide trend: Japanese and Chinese students outperforming all others. The very qualities celebrated in the larger community—hard work, enterprise, family stability—were seen as vices when displayed by Japanese residents.

Come war, paranoia became tinder for overheated emotions. Of all the ways a military assault on Duncan might be aided, the most difficult to anticipate was support from a so-called Japanese fifth column. Fifth column was the term given to supporters of an invasion who were supposedly working behind enemy lines. With their knowledge of the area's geography and critical industries, the resident Japanese, it was supposed, could cripple the valley before any invading force arrived. As with other Japanese communities along the coast, there was never any evidence—not any—to indicate Duncan's Japanese residents intended to support Japan's initiatives. But in Duncan, as elsewhere, the first victims of the war were facts.

Calls for removal of Duncan's Japanese began just days after the declaration of war against Japan. Heading the movement was the *Cowichan Leader*. Recounting how Singapore had fallen to Japan, in large part because of "vicious fifth-column activity by little brown men deemed to be very innocent and thus not molested by the authorities," the paper counselled swift internment of all local Japanese. To these editorial comments the paper added propaganda in the form of so-called reports from the war in China. Unsigned and undated, they featured accounts of atrocities inflicted by Japanese soldiers. One of these stories, "Murder Competition in Japanese Army," recounted a competition between two bloodthirsty Japanese soldiers: Sgt. Kato, "a little savage man with a face like a devil mask and flat black eyes," and his equally repulsive counterpart, Sgt. Fuji. Together, the two hacked, stabbed, bludgeoned and bayonetted their way through hundreds of victims. "This is how Japan makes war," the article concluded.

The patently purple story was all the more remarkable for the fact that its publication coincided with an event that might have signalled loyalty on the part of Japanese Canadians. After two years of trying in vain to enlist, Tony Kato was finally accepted into the Canadian Army—becoming the first Japanese Canadian in the country's armed forces.

Nor was the gossip mill lacking in hyperbole. In bars and restaurants, too, rumours took wing. At Waldie and Bremner's Motors, on Government Street, a crummy full of loggers said they had heard of an arms stash in Hillcrest. It was checked out but nothing was found. Mr. Aihoshi, owner of Duncan's Togo Shoe Repair, was said to be in contact with a fleet offshore via a powerful radio transmitter. One of the most persistent rumours was about an arms stash Japanese loggers were said to have hidden in caves in the Koksilah Range, 32 kilometres south of Duncan. A group was dispatched to the caves to investigate; they found emptiness.

Fear also prompted Duncan's business and community leaders to become involved. The Cowichan Branch of the Canadian Legion, the Elks and the Chamber of Commerce joined the City of Duncan in sending telegrams to Ottawa demanding the immediate internment of all Japanese on the coast. The normally staid Rotary Club added its voice: "To the Prime Minister: Rotary Club of Duncan urgently request immediate action to terminate Japanese fifth-column menace on this coast—urge removal of entire Japanese population to areas east of the Rockies and internment there—consider the situation here serious." The message was signed by Mayor E.W. Lee.

In the fear-fuelled environment even the slightest misdemeanour was seen as high treason. "Two Japanese Sugar Hoarding Cases Uncovered," trumpeted a *Leader* headline in early 1942. The paper revealed that sacks of rationed sugar were found stashed in two Japanese homes in Hillcrest. Never mind that the sugar had been sold to the Japanese by a local merchant. The *Leader* concluded the find was sinister in its implications: "It might be expected that Japanese who have little interest in the diversion of sugar for the production of explosives would have no scruples about hoarding sugar..."

Finally, after months of lobbying, the federal government acted. In early March a notice circulated demanding that all cameras and radios belonging to Japanese be handed in to the RCMP. Several weeks later, on the morning of March 19, vehicles belonging to Duncan's Japanese were impounded. Drivers convened at Duncan, then drove their vehicles under police escort to Willows Beach in Victoria. While they were waiting to leave, one of the Japanese was asked if he was annoyed at surrendering his car. He smiled and said: "It has to be done, I guess." Several of the vehicles had V for Victory stickers. Another had a placard that read: There Will Always Be An England.

Two Japanese-born Duncanites pose with their Canadian-born daughters on Ingram Street in the 1930s.
Left to right: Mrs. Nakashima and daughter Sayoko; Chiyoko Hashimoto, her mother, and Michiko Hashimoto.
Sayoko Kawaguchi collection

A similar air of mechanical inevitability surrounded the removal of Duncanites of Japanese descent a month later. Starting at 4:00 a.m. on April 21, all Japanese in the Cowichan Valley were escorted from their homes and taken to gathering points. The crowd at Duncan—thirty-six children, forty-nine men and thirty-four women—included the town's Japanese residents and some

from outlying areas. Single file and under the eye of a plainclothes RCMP officer, they boarded Vancouver Island Coach Lines busses. One of the last to go
was Mantaro Nagano. At 9:00 a.m. exactly, the coaches pulled out for
Chemainus where their human cargo would board a CPR steamer for
Vancouver and, ultimately, the BC Interior. By mid-morning Duncan was emp-
tied of Japanese blood—almost.

As the children of an English-born mother, Robert and Marion Kato
appeared to be incontestably white. When the war began Elizabeth had sought
from the government clarification of their status and received a letter stating
that her family was not to be interned. As well, many people knew that her
husband was overseas. Their loyalty was unquestionable. Yet on the streets and
in the classrooms, Robert and Marion were finding life miserable. For Robert,
life in 1938–41 was similar to that of almost any working-class Duncan boy. He
attended Duncan Elementary, joined Boy Scouts, listened to baseball on the
radio. His only connection with the Japanese side of his ancestry was occasional trips with his father to the homes of Japanese around Third Street,
where they would partake of a bath in a hot tub. Otherwise Robert regarded
the Japanese as play-enemies—like Indians in cowboys and Indians. He often
tore around the Duncan Elementary school grounds making machine gun
sounds with his mouth and strafing the make-believe enemy. During one game,
he and several friends staked out a building where they heard whispering. "It's

Marion and Robert Kato.
Robert Cato collection

Japs," Robert said, "they're planning sabotage." The door eventually opened and a dishevelled young couple emerged.

As soon as Canada declared war on Japan, however, Robert's ancestry was shoved in his face. Kids told him his family was going to be sent away with the rest of the community. "It began to leak in all around us," he recalled later. "We began to get harassed. People that were my friends were now teasing us. Then it got downright threatening." Children came up and said, "We know that you are going to be interned." Desperate, Elizabeth Kato tried appealing to public sentiment through a letter to the *Cowichan Leader*:

> Sir,—It has been brought to my attention that there has been some question and criticism as to the status of my children.
> The legal aspect of this matter was settled over a year ago, and again very recently in a personal reply from Ottawa. There are no government rules or regulations against these children.
> I answer for their loyalty and traditions. They have known no other influence than that of an English-born mother, who has believed in and taught them the best principles of democracy and good citizenship. That their father encouraged and lived these ideals also, is well known to those who knew him…
> In all, I must say that if loyalty, service and high principles do mean anything in this country, these children have every right to the freedom and equality to which they were born.

Her plea went unheard. Several months later the family moved to Vancouver. (Robert went on to have a distinguished career with the Canadian Navy. He retired to Ladysmith, where he restores military medals, including those of veterans from Duncan.)

The Japanese community in Duncan was never restored. Long before the war was over, their land and homes were sold, often for prices far below market value. Wooden chests were ransacked, hot tubs dismantled. The arable ground below Hospital Hill that had been the heart of "Jap Land" sat empty until 1943 when it was rented by QMS. That summer students planted potatoes. They named the area Galabooshta, from the title of a nonsense book.

The Post-War
Boom

Scene: A street in Duncan, circa 1953. A fisherman—crumpled felt hat
stuck full of flies, wicker creel slung over one shoulder, a shepherd's crook
clutched in one hand—strides along a sidewalk. Suddenly, Major L.C.
Rattray halts. On the street corner opposite he spots the portly figure of
Duncan Mayor James Wragg. Major Rattray fixes the mayor with a kestrel's
stare.

*Once the toniest hotel in
Duncan, the Tzouhalem
became known for its beer hall
atmosphere. BCARS E-00433*

Rattray: Wragg! Wragg! I say, WRAGG!

The mayor obediently trots across the road.

Wragg: Yes, Major Rattray?

Rattray: Look heah, Wragg. What's all this nonsense about the town getting parking meters?

Wragg: Oh come, Major Rattray, we've got to move with the times, ye know.

Rattray: What, what! Move with the times? These times? No, I'm damned if I do.

Maclean's, April 2, 1955

Duncan's Sikhs

The absence of an identifiable neighbourhood within city limits has never prevented Cowichan Valley Sikhs from taking a prominent role in Duncan's development. In the 1930s, especially, when other sawmills were shut down, it was Mayo Singh's lumber mill at Paldi that kept many Duncan families solvent. Herb Doman's massive lumber and logging company, Doman Industries, has had a similarly beneficial effect on the city since the 1970s.

Yet in the pre-war years the Sikhs, like the Japanese and the Chinese, were defined as much by restriction and prejudice as they were by their own culture. Sikhs could not vote nor could they enter many professions. A Sikh family who wanted to see a movie at the Station Street Odeon sat—along with Japanese, Chinese and Natives—in a special area on the balcony. A Sikh man who wanted a glass of beer was relegated to a corner of the Tzouhalem Hotel's beer parlour—unless he cut his hair. And if he did concede to cutting his hair, there was only one barber in Duncan who would do it. When that barber, who was Japanese, was interned, Sikhs who wanted a haircut had nowhere to go.

One local Sikh who found himself in such a conundrum was Karm Manak. Manak had come from India in 1921. In *Becoming Canadians: Pioneer Sikhs in Their Own Words*, Manak recalls going into one of the two remaining barbers in town and asking if he could get a haircut. The barber, who was sweeping the floor around empty chairs, said, "I'm busy now." So Manak bought out the barber's partner. "[T]hat way we got our family's and our people's hair cut there," he said. "That solved the problem."

A similarly entrepreneurial spirit prompted several local Sikhs to enlist Duncan Mayor James Wragg in an unusual lobbying effort. In 1947 Cowichan Valley industrialists Mayo Singh and Kapoor Singh and their lawyer travelled to Harrison Hot Springs, where the Union of British Columbia Municipalities

was having its annual convention, planning to speak to the convention about getting the right to vote. They were told the meeting was for municipal politicians only. So they invited the only two men they knew—Wragg and the mayor of Victoria—up to their hotel room, where they had stashed a case of Scotch. Kapoor Singh was not a drinker, but his lawyer advised him, "Your job is to offer anyone who comes in a drink." The Scotch had a salubrious effect on the politicians. Next day, the Sikhs were invited to speak to the convention. "These two men had hundreds of employees working for them," explained their lawyer. "Their workers were allowed to vote and these two mill owners could not vote because they were East Indian." A show of hands was held on the spot and it was decided that South Asians should be allowed to vote in local elections. Full franchise—the right to vote in all elections—was granted in September 1947.

There is no better index to the state of mind of post-war Duncan than the respective attitudes of Major Laurence Chapman Rattray and Mayor James Chesterfield Wragg. Rattray, the self-declared spokesperson for the aging community of Longstockings still clustered around the town, deeply resented the changes he saw taking place: the decline of churches, the ascendance of a Chamber of Commerce business-first mentality and a migration that made the town's population blossom from 1,500 in 1939 to 3,000 in the mid-1950s. Wragg, on the other hand, was typical of the emerging merchant class: boisterous, confident, more concerned with power than pedigree, more interested in capital than the number of letters a man sported behind his name. The two men knew and respected each other but in outlook they were as different as pipe tobacco and chewing gum.

Mayo Singh, pictured here in 1930, came from India in 1906. He worked on farms and in lumber mills before starting his own mill at Paldi in 1918. CVM N998.11.31

In appearance, at least, Duncan in the early 1950s still resembled a Wold-on-Thames English country village. Crusty old Colonel Blimp types prowled the shops, many still dressed as if preparing for a day under the blazing skies

of the tropics. Cricket Club news dominated the sports pages of the *Cowichan Leader*, gala balls at the Agricultural Hall remained the premier social event of the local calendar. The town had the aura of an outpost of Empire.

In truth, though, the heyday of the Longstocking was waning. From the late 1930s population of an estimated 2,000-plus, they were reduced to less than half that number. Fears of a Japanese invasion in 1942 had set many Longstockings packing for home. Britain's post-war devaluation of the pound, which effectively halved their pensions, fuelled the exodus. Age conquered others. Of the remainder, many were living lampoons of an earlier age.

Typical of the surviving Longstockings was Major Rattray. A strapping, handsome man, he frequently dressed in a kilt, which gave full stage to his well-defined calf muscles and great hairy knees. Scots by birth, he had served in the Boer War and with the King's Royal Rifles in the First World War before retiring to Duncan to fish and grow roses. He was a stickler for the privileges of rank. He said "Sir" to men several ranks senior to himself and expected "Sir" from men several ranks lower—even if they were the mayor of Duncan.

Rattray shared with many Longstockings an annoying everyday arrogance. For one, he disdained all forms of traffic. With no more than a shake of his shepherd's crook, he would stride across a busy street, steadfastly ignoring the jumbled vehicles in his wake. Rattray once drove his car into the path of an oncoming train. The crash demolished the vehicle. When asked what happened Rattray said, "I don't know why it didn't stop. I honked at it." Aging and infirm, warriors like Rattray and the nearly blind Dopping-Hepenstal were reduced to fulminating about the glory days of the "Empah," when there weren't even cars, let alone parking meters.

Before they evaporated from the Duncan social scene, however, the Longstockings staged one last hurrah for the Empire and everything it stood for. This was the proposed blockade of a royal procession that gained Duncan worldwide attention.

In 1951, the Cowichan Valley's Longstocking community was stunned by the news that the recently married Princess Elizabeth and Duke of Edinburgh would visit Vancouver Island but drive past Duncan. Royal processions had always included Duncan on their itinerary. On this occasion, however, Duncanites were informed that the royal entourage would speed straight through from Victoria to Nanaimo. So they turned to the genial mayor of the town.

Mayor Jimmy Wragg had always had a friendly relationship with the area's Longstockings. As the former owner of a bakery he often counselled British emigrants recently arrived from the Empire's outposts about daily Duncan life. "I used to feel sorry for the ladies just in from China, India and Africa when I was running my shop," he recounted. "They had been used to a houseful of native servants, and they were lost when they got to Canada. Why, they couldn't even make a rice pudding. They'd come in to the shop with all the mixings—rice, sugar, milk and so on—in a basin and plead with me to make a pudding. I always did."

Soldier, baker, landlord, Mayor James Chesterfield Wragg. This drawing by Mort Graham was published in 1951.

Brooksby Isobel's Choice (No. 53789)

As a money-savvy businessman, Duncan Mayor Jimmy Wragg was aware of agriculture's importance to the town's economy. That's why, when a $2,000 prize cow developed pneumonia at the Cowichan Fall Fair, Wragg called out the Duncan Volunteer Fire Department. The animal needed air; the department had an inhalator. The machine happened to be designed for humans but Wragg didn't care. With air blown into her lungs, the valuable cow soon recovered.

Agriculture has been the middle child of Duncan's economic family in the twentieth century. Not boisterous like logging, not flamboyant like the Longstockings, it contributed steadily to the town's growth. With a third of Vancouver Island's agricultural land in the Cowichan Valley, local farmers produced beef, poultry, eggs, pork, holly, Christmas trees, potatoes, sheep, milk and honey. The largest crops of asparagus in BC were grown at Cowichan Bay. Nearby James Bros. Seed Farm was once the biggest seed producer in Canada. Crosland's sweet pea seed farm was the oldest in the Dominion, a distinction that earned the Crosland family coverage in the *London Times*, the *Field*, the *Home and Garden* and newspapers in South Africa and Australia. ("I do not know where Duncan is," confessed one correspondent, "but I know it is home of the sweet pea.")

Barkley's red-polled cattle exhibit was a feature of an early Cowichan Fall Fair. BCARS E-00434

Agriculture warranted major coverage in the *Cowichan Leader*, too. During the 1910s the paper ran front-page updates on the ranking of local chickens at a prestigious annual international egg laying contest. The contest, run under the auspices of the Provincial Department of Agriculture in Victoria, pitted the nation's best birds against those of other countries. Duncan area chickens always lived up to the town's billing as "The Egg Basket of Canada." In 1915, for example,

Duncanite E.W. Estridge's six top white leghorns beat out some twenty-eight competitors by laying a total of 1,122 eggs in twelve months. Five of the top ten positions also went to Cowichan birds—evoking from a local poet a lengthy doggerel which concluded:

> Then, hail; all hail to the Cowichan hen,
> The greatest blessing of all to men;
> Throw up our hats and emit a howl
> For the persevering barnyard fowl,
> Corn may be king, but it is plainly seen,
> That the Cowichan hen is the Cowichan queen.

In 1922 John Newell Evans's dairy cow No. 53789 achieved brief celebrity status. More commonly known as Brooksby Isobel's Choice, the Cowichan-born and -raised Holstein set a Canadian record by producing 11,606 kilograms of milk in one year. She narrowly beat the previous champion, the highly regarded Calamity Snow Mechthilde (No.40460) of Ontario.

The offspring of a bull named BC Choice Goods, Brooksby Isobel's Choice had shown such little promise as a heifer that her original owner couldn't sell her at auction. Evans swapped a Jersey cow for her. In her second year Brooksby Isobel's Choice produced a respectable 4,767 kilograms of milk. Then, fattened on Evans's rich Cowichan Lake Road pastures, she more than doubled her output a year later to set the national record. "Cowichan cows have been making wonderful records for some time," boasted the *Leader*. "The owner of a cow that sends the record a few points higher certainly earns his passport to the hall of fame."

During the 1940s and 1950s, the railroad was kept busy moving feed to the creamery and logs through town. Note the five-wide tracks. CVM 987.06.1.2

Longstocking men complicated Wragg's life, too. Fresh from the river, they slogged into his shop every day and announced, "Wragg, old boy! A present for you," and heaved a large salmon on his counter. Some days more than a dozen fish were piled in the shop. Wragg couldn't give them away. "I got sick of the sight of salmon," he recalled. "I used to wonder, 'Wragg, what are you? A baker or a salmon exchange?'"

Jimmy Wragg had the kind of background most Longstockings would have written right out of their genealogy. His father, Thomas Benjamin Wragg, kept the Marquis of Granby pub in Devon, England. On the day Jimmy Wragg was born under the roof of the pub itself, Mr. Wragg senior won £200 on a race-horse named Chesterfield. So he named the new son James Chesterfield Wragg. "I was named for a racehorse and I've always played my luck since," Jimmy Wragg liked to say. "It's never let me down."

Luck got Jimmy Wragg out of England, too. He was working as a bakery boy when his uncle tipped him about a horse named Christmas Daisy. So Jimmy put down half a week's wages. Christmas Daisy paid 100 to 7 and Wragg bought passage on a steamer bound for Canada. He worked all over the western provinces, as cook, logger, farmhand, kitchen help. World War I took him back to Europe, where he was injured twice in action and finished with the rank of sergeant. When he returned to Canada he tried a job cooking in an Alice Arm logging camp but quit when a gang of drunken loggers burst into the kitchen at midnight and stole seventy-five lemon pies. He and his wife Ella bought a bakery in Cobble Hill, worked hard and prospered, and after they had built up the business they sold it and moved to a luxurious three-bedroom home at 940 Island Highway.

Across from the post office an empty lot went up for sale for $5,500. Wragg talked the owners into halving the lot and the price. Then he built a two-storey building and opened Wragg's Bakery. The first creature to walk in, he later recalled, was a black cat. When the day was over the bakery had taken in an astounding $137 and the cash register was ticking like an overheated motor. From that time on the Wraggs worked fourteen and fifteen hours a day. As fast as they made money they spent it on real estate. Jimmy Wragg built an apartment block on Government Street and apartments all over town. At one time he owned fourteen stores and was the biggest individual taxpayer in town. He collected rent in cash, and he paid cash for everything from flour for his store to the new car he bought each year.

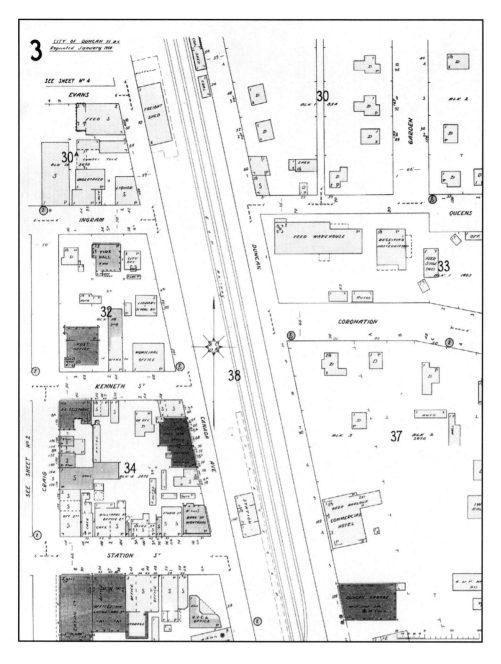

As long as he was a working man, Wragg had little time for charities and organizations. Come the Second World War, however, he took on seven jobs: alderman, trustee, official in charge of women agricultural workers, St. John ambulance worker, civil defence warden, director of the hospital and regional director of the aircraft detection unit from Port Renfrew to the Malahat. To save fuel for the war effort he left his car parked in the driveway of his home and walked to work each day.

Wragg's ambition made him appealing to a new generation of community and business leaders looking for a mayor to steward Duncan in the post-war

Station Street and Canada Avenue, 1954. CVM 996.6.4.1 Sheet 3

years. This generation included many young veterans freshly returned from Europe or the Pacific where, in their early twenties, they had commanded destroyers, aircraft and tanks, led battalions into battle, fought hard, won a war. Jack Davie, decorated for his role in military landings in North Africa, Sicily and France, partnered with a whip-smart young veteran named David Ricardo Williams and took over a law firm. Will Dobson, who did two tours with the RAF's Bomber Command, became *Cowichan Leader* editor. Energetic and confident, these and hundreds of other Duncan-area veterans started businesses and joined community organizations. They took over the town.

Logs and Loggers

As the merchant centre of a timber-rich valley, Duncan has often been associated with logs and loggers. When Lake Cowichan companies shipped out 30- and 36-metre poles for hydro lines spanning the Mississippi River, Duncan got the credit. When BC Forest Products camps set records for safety, Duncan loggers made the news.

In truth, the city's relationship with logging was anything but first-hand. Lake Cowichan produced logs. Chemainus had the sawmill. And (later) Crofton produced pulp and paper. If not for the rail cars of logs that were parked on the four- and five-wide sidings that existed in 1940s Duncan, a visitor could easily have mistaken the town for a farming settlement.

Duncan's association with forestry is more administrative. Ever since the late 1930s, when the International Woodworkers of America was formed, Local 1-80 has had an office in the city. Several forest companies have had offices in the downtown, too. The presence of the IWA became a centre of concern in the 1940s, when a division in the union, known as "The Big Split," resulted in a break-in at the union office. Unbeknowst to the disgruntled union members, however, a *Leader* editor stood on the street outside. He calmly wrote down the items being removed—filing cabinets, desks, records—and printed the story in the next issue. Relations between the union, which didn't like having its laundry washed in public, and the paper, which was definitely unsympathetic to labour, were strained for some time afterward.

The King's Daughters Hospital was another Duncan institution associated with logging. The hospital's seemingly endless expansions were a result of the increasing number of accidents in the woods. In just one week in 1930, for example, the following mishaps were recorded:

Jun Long, faller. Skull fractured by falling snag.

S. Inouye, faller. Shoulder and upper arm broken by limb.

Alan Munroe, rigger. Fell on back.

J. Laird, hooker. Pelvis fractured by snag.

Hemmer Dahl, chokerman. Chest crushed by log.

The need to transport men from the woods to the hospital in Duncan led to another local service: the ambulance. Prior to 1926, an injured logger was brought to town in a company vehicle—often the back of a pickup truck. This gave rise to the frequently heard comment that if an accident failed to kill a logger then the ride to Duncan would. In 1926 the Cowichan District Ambulance Service was formed. It was run by J.A. Kyle, an ex-E&N railway man. His first ambulance was a former hearse, and the first passenger was a Miss Day, of Duncan. She paid $3.00 for a ride to the hospital. Eventually Kyle's sons, Bert and Val, took over the service. They carried hundreds of injured loggers to hospital, as well as victims of domestic and motor vehicle accidents. In the mid-1950s, the Kiwanis Club took over the ambulance service. They ran it until the late 1960s, when the Cowichan Valley Regional District assumed responsibility. The CVRD, in turn, handed operations to the BC Ambulance Service on July 1, 1974.

An increase in the use of trucks instead of railways to move logs put pressure on Duncan's streets. This 1932 Ford logging truck was photographed outside Duncan Garage in 1935.
CVM 990.06.2.11

In 1946 a conflict between the newly returned veterans and city hall turned ugly. Duncan council, headed by Mayor George Savage, selected a new city clerk: Gordon Berry, an Ontarian who had not served in the war. Members of the business community, many of whom were also members of the Canadian Legion, objected. When council would not reverse their decision, Legion members stormed city hall. A Legion spokesman said council was flouting the national policy of hiring veterans. Mayor Savage tried to placate the visitors. The highlight of the evening was when long-time councillor William Evans reminded the veterans that they had gone overseas of their own choice, no one had forced them. He said they should take their place in the community as good citizens. Mayor Savage tried to calm the donnybrook that followed Evans's comments. He said the alderman had expressed himself unfortunately and he was sure the words sounded worse than intended. As the *Leader* noted, "The veterans were not appeased."

Outraged, the Legion encouraged Wragg to run for mayor in the next election. He did, and was returned four times. Neither Savage nor Evans held office again.

Mayor Wragg completely overhauled the machinery of city government. During the eight years he was in office, Duncan bought new vehicles for public works; pushed forward a streets improvement plan and launched a lighting improvement plan; bought its own waterworks; built a new $45,000 firehall, fully equipped; put in sewers; acquired a new garbage truck and streamlined the collection system; built a new city hall; and introduced a contract system for public works. He stepped on a few toes to accomplish so much, but even those who didn't like Jimmy Wragg admitted he was one of the best mayors the town had ever had. He got things done.

When Wragg heard of the royal entourage's plans to bypass Duncan he wrote a letter of protest to Buckingham Palace. They replied that the timetable could not be changed. He then went on radio to announce that he would "throw a human chain across the road" and halt the royal procession. In the context of the times, his pronouncement was akin to insurrection. Yet the call to arms appealed to old colonels and brigadiers. For this operation, at least, they offered to put themselves under *Sergeant* Wragg's command. Newspapers on both sides of the Atlantic published photos showing Mayor Wragg and his supporters linking arms across the highway in illustration of how they intended to carry out the threat. "Personally, I think that the Princess is more interested in meeting common people than in mixing with politicians in Victoria," Wragg was quoted as saying.

On the day of the royal visit, 10,000 valley residents gathered in the town to see what would happen. When the Duke of Edinburgh, who was driving, approached the outskirts of town, he grinned and slowed to walking speed. The blockade was called off because there was no need: everybody got a good view of the dashing royal newlyweds, and a few bystanders exchanged pleasantries with the young princess. At a reception in Nanaimo later that day Wragg was introduced to Her Majesty. "That was quite an exciting reception you gave us in Duncan today," she said.

Years later Wragg confessed that the idea of the blockade wasn't his in the first place. It had been whispered in his ear by a stout little woman in tweed skirt and sensible brogues: Norah Denny.

The Highway

Of all the changes that occurred in and around post-war Duncan—the increase in automobile traffic, the rise of plazas and the development of Reserve land—the most significant was the 1951 rerouting of the Island Highway. Where the old highway had followed a serpentine path into the city centre, the new road funnelled north- and southbound traffic straight through Duncan on an expanded York Road. The change replaced a quiet suburban area with a ribbon of strip development and very nearly killed the downtown core.

The Island Highway had not changed significantly in four decades. A vehicle travelling north emerged from Koksilah, crossed the E&N Railway tracks, then followed the river to the White Bridge. It entered Duncan proper at an intersection marked by several service stations and, on the northeast corner, the Cowichan Merchants building. The vehicle then swung hard left and followed the highway past Chinatown, the liquor store and up through a timbered area of Indian Reserve, past Queen Margaret's School and out of town.

By any measure, the route was tortuous. For the increasing number of heavy trucks on the road it was also dangerous. Cowichan Bay-bound logging trucks loaded with boomsticks had a particular challenge negotiating the corner at Government Street. More than once the gas pumps at Wilson & Cabeldu's Shell Oil Station at the northwest corner were wiped out by an articulating overhang of logs. As early as the 1930s, local and provincial politicians were talking about the pressing need to do something about the highway.

The Cowichan River washed out the Island Highway south of Duncan in 1935. Problems with the route prompted construction of the new highway. CVM N995.08.23.36

In 1948 E.C. Carson, then provincial minister of public works, announced that the government was going to make changes and invited comments from local politicians. The town quickly divided into two camps: those who wanted to fiddle with the existing route—by angling the highway through Reserve land until it intersected the Island Highway around Queen Margaret's School—and those who wanted it directed through town on a new route. Arguing that the island's skyrocketing population would soon make even a revamped older route inadequate, proponents of the new route suggested the highway cross the river south of the Black Bridge, then cut straight through town on any north-south road—Duncan Street, Festubert Street and York Road were often mentioned—then head northward skirting Somenos Lake. The drawback of this route was expense: the sprawling river would have to be dyked and huge approaches created on the low-lying river banks.

In 1949 the provincial government announced it was going ahead with the York Road option. Construction took the best part of the year. What was once a restful neighbourhood with a school and a mood all its own was transformed into a throughway. Businesses dependent on traffic displaced York Road homes. Bill Vanderlip built a gas station across from Long's Grocery. Colonel Ross renovated Ashdown Henry Green's Kilninta into the Silver Bridge Inn. The York Road neighbourhood, as it was called, was transformed into the Strip—an interlocking web of food outlets, stores and gas stations that had the characteristics of what urban geographers call "placelessness"; it could be Duncan, it could be Campbell River, it could be Trent, Ontario.

The rerouting of the highway had almost the opposite effect on downtown Duncan. Like a tree whose taproot has been severed, the core area stopped growing and actually faded. Shoddy shops and For Rent signs were common in the 1970s and early 1980s. The imbalance threatened to capsize the town's traditional three-way Hospital Hill–downtown core–townsite configuration. It may well have, too, had not city council capitalized on an opportunity and renovated the post office building for city hall. The renovation sparked a resurgence of interest in the old town area. The buildings were varied and interesting. Compared to the architectural monoculture on the highway, downtown Duncan was a rich mix of old and new, like the forest it replaced. Since the late 1980s, the old town has been one of the features to draw travellers off the Island Highway.

Until the Island Highway was rerouted in 1951, Long's Grocery at the northwest corner of York Road and Trunk Road anchored the quiet York Road neighbourhood.
CVM N998.9.1.5

Asked why he didn't return to Scotland to fetch his inheritance, Robert Hew Ferguson-Pollock said that his wife Margaret "didn't want me to." Note the jigsaw puzzles. Jack Long photo, CVM 998.10.2.1

In 1955 *Maclean's* magazine dispatched McKenzie Porter, a Toronto writer, to Duncan to see if there was still life coursing through the town's once legendary British community. Porter found the community in decline, all right, but also in decay. Once the home of such stalwarts as Phillipps-Wolley, Duncan now sheltered men and women who had fled England after a breach of convention. He cited the examples of Walter Rudkin, an English gardener who married the daughter of a duke and raised apples in the Cowichan Valley; Teddy Hicks-Beach, the son of a Chancellor of the Exchequer in the British Parliament, allegedly cut off by his father for marrying William and Clara Jaynes's daughter, Louise; and Miss Bowes-Lyon, a member of the Queen Mother's family who married E.W. Cole, a former choir boy twenty years her junior, then settled in the Duncan area and raised pedigree dogs. "After dressing for dinner in the bush for nearly a century," wrote Porter, "Canada's most die-hard community of old-fashioned British aristocrats is finally petering out."

Porter interviewed Major Rattray, Mayor Wragg and others, but to illustrate just how far Duncan's once toney English community had fallen, he focussed on the story of Robert Hew Ferguson-Pollock. Ferguson-Pollock was a second-generation Longstocking who could trace every one of his male ancestors to the eleventh century. Six-foot-four, with a head of ocean-grey hair and a notorious aversion to bathing, Ferguson-Pollock was a sometime mate on coastal tugs when, in 1951, he inherited Pollock Castle, a sprawling estate and nineteen farms around Newton Means, Scotland. Ferguson-Pollock and his wife Margaret, a former barmaid, ordered lawyers to sell the estate and castle and send the furniture to their manor in Duncan.

The Ferguson-Pollocks eventually frittered the fortune away and were reduced to selling salmon door to door in Duncan, clad in ragged, smelly clothes and dime store flip-flops. When Porter interviewed them, however, much of the furniture was intact. The house was jammed with unbelievable treasures: Chippendale chairs, a whole Hepplewhite suite, a Jacobean solitaire table and a Queen Anne cabinet full of thirteenth century Venetian glass, claymores, ancient duelling pistols and shields of highland chieftains. "A dozen Persian rugs are kept rolled up because there is no place to lay them," Porter wrote, incredulously. Yet despite this wealth, the Ferguson-Pollocks passed their days at a great oak dining table dating from Charles I, working at their favourite pastime: jigsaw puzzles.

Porter's article, "The Last Stronghold of the Longstockings," was published in *Maclean's* in April 1955. Local newsstands could not keep the issue on the shelves. Never before had Duncanites seen their community etched in such a light. And what they saw they did not recognize. Their cries of outrage were enough to draw the attention of the Victoria press, who sent a reporter to check out the legitimacy of Porter's claims. Everyone the reporter interviewed said Porter had drawn on his imagination for the story. The ancient duelling pistol referred to in the article, said Mrs. Ferguson-Pollock, was actually a Long John Silver capgun that her husband had bought in a Duncan department store toyland. Mayor Wragg read the piece and was convulsed with laughter. The last word went to Major Rattray. After reading Porter's article he denied everything written about him. "Pure invention," he said, chortling around his pipe, "a lot of jolly nonsense."

The Reinvention of Duncan

Three Duncan institutions: the
Agricultural Hall, Strawberry
Hill and the Tzouhalem Hotel,
c. 1963. The hall and the hotel
have been demolished.
CVM 987.10.1.52

IN THE POST-1950 MEMORIES of the people of Duncan three events seem to
stand out—the demolition of Chinatown in 1970; a mayor's fractious and
unsuccessful attempt, in 1978, to have the city vote itself out of existence; and
the relocation—ordered by the Supreme Court of Canada in 1958—of the
Cowichan Agricultural Society, which for sixty-two years had occupied 2
hectares of Reserve land on the south side of Government Street, between
Strawberry Hill and the railway tracks. The Agricultural Grounds, as the area
was called, was Duncan's recreational and social pivot. On its fields residents
played soccer, football, rugby, track and field; in the massive barn-like hall they
danced, staged dog, cat, poultry, baby and flower shows, held meetings and
conferences, played badminton and basketball.

King's Daughters Summer Show. Duncan. 1915

The Agricultural Grounds were the offspring of an autumn event staged by St. Peter's Anglican Church in the 1860s. The Harvest Home was a give-thanks celebration marking the end of the frenzied summer growing season. In 1868 a competitive aspect was added to the event when Reverend Reece suggested that parishioners bring along their best produce for judging. From this competition the Cowichan Exhibition was created. The Exhibition moved from St. Peter's to Maple Bay; then, in 1888, to an area leased by the Exhibition's parent body, the Cowichan Agricultural Society, from Charley Quitquartin, a Cowichan Native. Two buildings were put up on the property: in 1888, a cubical wood structure that became known as the Armoury, for many years home to military reserve units; and in 1914, the Agricultural Hall, a slightly less inelegant three-storey brick and wood structure that fronted onto Government Street.

All who grew up in early- to mid-century Duncan have some memory of the Agricultural Hall. They recall trying to loft badminton birdies to the ceiling's unachievable heights, listening to interminable political speeches or, especially, attending the gala balls. Several times a year, from pre-World War I to well into the 1950s, live bands set up on the left side of the great hall and struck

From baby showers to flower shows, the Agricultural Hall was the centre of Duncan's social life for six decades. This photograph was taken in 1915. BCARS 77822

Cowichan Merchants (later Eaton's department store) looms behind Kate Buckmaster as she guides her mount, Bonnie Doone, over a jump at the fairgrounds, c. 1937. CVM 998.10.5.1

up music for dances that lasted until two or three in the morning. Classy, well-behaved affairs, they gave average Duncanites—loggers, mechanics, farmers, merchants—a chance to shed trappings of their everyday lives and recast themselves as aristocrats. One of the most remarkable transformations was effected on Elvin Waldie, a former high rigger who went into auto sales after a fall from the summit of a spar tree left him with a steel plate in his head. Polished black shoes barely touching the floor, coat and tails trailing gracefully behind, Waldie spun across the great expanse of dance floor with the panache of a Viennese prince.

The Cowichan Exhibition was the central event on Cowichan's calendar. From all over the district gardeners and farmers lugged their produce and animals for display: giant gourds, Cox's orange pippin apples, barred rock chickens, jars of plum jam, honey, pickles, pies, children's art, handicrafts. The valley was like a giant garden and the fair was the public pantry where it showed off its goods.

The land continued to be used until the late 1940s, when the Indian Affairs Department responded to a claim by the Cowichan Tribes and took the matter to court. The Exchequer supported the Cowichans' charge—that the last two renewals on the Agricultural Grounds had been granted without order in council approval and therefore the contract was worthless. After a long and costly legal skirmish, the Supreme Court of Canada forced the Cowichan Agricultural Society to move to Clement Street, near the Cowichan Exhibition Grounds, located on the site of the Evans farm. The Agricultural Hall was demolished in 1968. Of the sprawling structure not a trace remains.

The Duncan Volunteer Fire Department

There is no secret to predicting large fires in the City of Duncan. They always follow the appointment of a new fire chief. Hence, the undertaker's building caught fire just after George Sanderson was made chief, the Midway Hotel started billowing smoke following Jim Morrisey's appointment, the K&R Grocery blazed when Glenn Mackie took over and the Knights of Pythias Hall burned soon after Joe Chaster became chief. Following the same superstitious logic, then, it was inevitable that something big would come along following the appointment of Vern Jones as fire chief in mid-April 1969.

Duncan firefighters at work, 1968. Cowichan Leader

CAPTAIN CHARLIE CLARK, DVFD, is shown playing water on a large storage bin 12 hours after the outbreak at the Co-op. Services plant at 2:30 a.m. Sunday. Laminated construction of the bin made it remarkably flame and heat resistant.

A week after Jones's appointment, a motorist was driving through downtown at 2:30 a.m. when he noticed an orange flame emerging from the Cowichan Creamery. The towering wood structure rising from the corner of Duncan Street and Queens Road was a local landmark and Duncan's only true in-city industry. Twice the creamery had burned—in 1911 and again in 1948—and twice it was rebuilt. With its dusty wooden rafters and unfrequented storage rooms, it was the embodiment of a fire trap. The motorist stopped at a pay phone and called the fire department.

The Duncan Volunteer Fire Department had changed a lot since the days when a bucket of water and wooden ladder were considered state-of-the-art equipment. One of the first improvements was the purchase of a 1914 Cadillac, which was able to speed firefighters everywhere except to Hospital Hill homes, where the vehicle required a push to get it up the grade. The Cadillac was replaced with more modern trucks operating from a converted barn on Ingram Street.

The firefighters had improved, too. Duncan's first generation trained in single-purpose tasks: nozzle men, chemical men, couplers and so on. Under the new arrangement, firefighters were skilled in handling any equipment and knew how to fight fires like their professional counterparts in larger cities.

Charlie Clark was typical of the fire department's new breed. A mechanic by trade, Clark had arrived in Duncan from Prince Edward Island in early 1953. A year later the chimney in his Alderlea Street home caught fire and he came face to face with the department's charismatic chief, George Sanderson. Sanderson had an eye for versatile men and soon recruited Clark, who learned every task in the department.

Charlie Clark was at home when the call came that the creamery was ablaze. By the time he had dressed and got downtown, flames were licking out of the structure's windows. "When I got there it was going pretty good," he recalled. Fellow members Tom Clark and Jack Davie arrived in Truck No. 3, an International that was considered the workhorse of the department. Vern Jones, the newly appointed chief, told the threesome to cover the back of the building. The blaze was so hot it blew the windows out of a nearby house and popped the safety valves on gas tanks, which jetted flame. Molten iron from the galvanized roof dripped into the building, setting off a series of grain dust explosions. Clark and Davies connected a firehose to a hydrant but the hose broke, sending the severed end whipping around lethally. By the time they got the hose fixed, the creamery was an inferno. The men's challenge was to keep the blaze from leapfrogging to other buildings. They battled the fire for hours. Only later did they discover that a shack where they were stationed warehoused 15 tons of highly explosive sodium nitrate fertilizer.

The fire ended the creamery's presence in the City of Duncan; the enterprise moved to the Trans-Canada Highway and operated as Cowichan Co-operative Service until 1988, when it was taken over by a private company.

As for the Duncan Fire Department, it continued to improve, moving into a new fire hall on Duncan Street in 1984. The building features a recreation area, a museum and a well-equipped training room. All of which, it is hoped, will keep the fire chief from moving on.

Wah Sing Chow was holidaying in California in the spring of 1962 when his heart gave out. He was sixty-four years old. His sudden and unexpected death contrasted with the decade-long demise of Duncan's Chinatown, the remnants of which only disappeared in 1970. What was called "one of the best Chinatown blocks anywhere in small-town North America" was replaced with a concrete building housing a seniors' centre and library, and the courthouse. Where the Pekin cafe stood is now a gravel parking lot.

As part of a nationwide urban renewal plan in the early 1960s, the provincial government began buying land on which Chinatown was built. The government was looking to increase its presence in Duncan and the dilapidated area seemed an ideal site. Many second- and third-generation Chinese were pursuing careers in larger cities. Of Wah Sing Chow's eight children, for example, only one son, Edmond, would remain in Duncan; the rest dispersed to Vancouver, Victoria, Washington state, California and Ontario. (Several ex-Duncanites achieved some status: Edwin Chow, Wah Sing Chow's third son and a retired Canadian Army captain and pharmacist, became mayor of Petawawa, Ontario; Kenny Chang was a popular Los Angeles sportscaster; and David Chan, a former Kenneth Street greengrocer, became a top photographer with *Playboy*.)

As for the resident population of Chinatown, there were only a half-dozen aging bachelors living in the leaking and ancient buildings. They were given the opportunity to move to new accommodation in the Chinese School on First Street.

Not everyone agreed that the demolition should proceed. Several members of the 1970 city council belatedly suggested transforming Chinatown into a West Coast Chinese museum. But the city risked losing the Centennial grant for a new library and senior citizens' centre if the area was not completely

Although Chinatown's destruction has been lamented, there was little support for its preservation in the 1960s.
CVM 1988.3.9.7

cleared. The provincial government would not allow the buildings to remain, nor would it finance moving them. Tenders were called for their destruction.

The contract to take down the four-building core of Chinatown was awarded to a contractor named Randy Streit, and the dismantling took three months. In the attics of the old buildings, Streit and his crew found the stored belongings of long-vanished tenants. There were kit bags and suitcases containing caulk boots, runners, a suit of Sunday clothes, shaving gear and a teapot. In the cobwebby attic Streit found over two hundred buckets hanging from the rafters—each, apparently, hung to intercept a leak.

While the crew worked on the buildings, many passersby stopped to watch. Artists gathered to paint the last remnants of Duncan's Chinatown. Young observers, especially, often commented on what a shame it was to destroy the heritage buildings. Streit told a journalist he had begun to feel personally responsible for the demolition. He eventually salvaged what he could of the buildings and moved them piecemeal to an empty lot south of town. They exist as part of Whippletree Junction.

What is Chinatown's legacy? For half a century the enclave was a flying buttress in the structure of Duncan's economy. The town prospered on Chinese Canadian acumen and sweat. When Chinatown vanished, the town as a whole was struck by what it had lost. The suddenly acquired sense of architectural history may have fuelled efforts to save Duncan's post office and train station and led to the enacting of heritage status legislation.

As for Chinatown's leaders, they exist only in memory and keepsake. Sue Lem Bing was 100 years old when he died in 1989. His Lewis Street home was demolished but his rhododendron lives on in a lush Maple Bay yard, blossoming purple every spring. Wah Sing Chow's home was also knocked down, replaced with an apartment for the elderly. Of his sizable estate the most valuable item, in non-economic terms, is his braided hair, which he happily lopped off when the Ching Dynasty ended in China in 1911. It is locked in a wooden box in his daughter's home in the USA.

Ever since Duncan's tax rate surged past that of the rate of neighbouring North Cowichan in 1916, there have been intermittent calls for a reunion of the municipality and the city. The calls became more frequent in the 1960s and 1970s, when growth in the municipality of North Cowichan made the border between city and municipality indistinguishable.

In 1978, then City of Duncan Mayor Ken Paskin mounted a campaign to unite the two political entities. The British-born Paskin had little time for the minutiae of small-town city politics. He liked to get things done and then check with his councillors about what they thought. This often led to news-making conflagrations. City clerk Paul Douville diplomatically said at Paskin's death that the former mayor was "a very exciting person to work with."

The facades of several Chinatown buildings were reconstructed at Whippletree Junction. Tom Henry photo

In a series of reports and speeches throughout spring and early summer, Paskin and North Cowichan Mayor George Whittaker lobbied in support of amalgamation. The reasons, as Paskin outlined, were primarily duplication of services. The administration of Duncan—everything from mayor to city clerk to the maintenance staff—were carbon copied in North Cowichan. The most graphic case of overlap was in fire protection. The North Cowichan Volunteer Fire Department was just a few doors down from the City of Duncan Volunteer Fire Department. Such examples, said Paskin, were a "disgraceful waste of taxpayer's money."

What started out as an exercise in comparative public finances soon turned into a vitriolic campaign resembling the Hatfield–McCoy feud. On one side were Paskin and the like-minded North Cowichan Mayor George Whittaker. On the other were the anti-amalgamation forces, which included most of Duncan's aldermen. One of the most determined of these was Alderman Doug Barker, who denounced possible savings as a red herring and declared that a union of the two political bodies would leave Duncanites without a voice. Paskin took the criticism personally and told the press that it might be a good idea if Barker "considered becoming a candidate in the Gong Show, April Fool's Day." The rest of Duncan's aldermen rallied around Barker and voted to censure the renegade mayor.

In late June 1978, the issue of amalgamation was put to the voters. Overall, the combined vote in Duncan and North Cowichan was 3,239 against amalgamation and 1,181 for. In Duncan the vote was against amalgamation 490 votes to 235. The heat of the campaign was in large part responsible for Paskin losing his seat a year later. Commenting on the vote, Alderman (later Mayor) Doug Barker said, "I'm glad it's over. The people have had their say and now it should be forgotten."

In every decade for over a century men and women have walked Duncan's streets who were somehow…different. Characters, they were called. They dressed poorly, talked to themselves, carried their few belongings in shopping carts or bags. Sometimes tragic, always odd, they led lives so at variance with the norm that they became temporal landmarks, giving faces and names to eras in Duncan's history. City residents who cannot remember what the York Road neighbourhood looked like, for example, can recall in detail the potato-skin texture of Chew Deb's face, or the fetid odours of Oliver Pipe's sweat-stained jacket, or the warmth of a greasy dime that Happy dispensed from his trouser pockets.

Deb and Pipe and Happy were the more prominent of a half-dozen characters who have roamed Duncan's streets since the Second World War. Deb was a near-legendary bootlegger who was disfigured when dynamite he was drying in an oven exploded. His hunched-over figure was a familiar sight around the back of Chinatown, where he ferried bottles from the liquor store to waiting Natives prohibited by law from buying liquor.

Oliver Pipe's turf was the cenotaph. A short, compact man with broad shoulders, he knitted caps using string and nails. He was once a superb axeman, capable of shouldering two fresh-cut rail ties at a time. He also wrote poetry which he sold in booklets for beer money. One poem was an ode to his hat and included the lines:

> Now, old hat, your day is past,
> You've covered my head from winter's blast,
> Sheltered my head lacking of brain,
> Keep it dry through snow and rain.

The bespectacled, gumbooted Chinese man who shuffled around town in the 1970s is remembered by many Duncanites as Happy. Happy was the common name; in the Chinese community he was called Ox-tail, a reference to his soup preference. Left over from the days of Chinese labourers, Happy shuffled about town in black pants, black gumboots and black jacket, doling out lint-clad coins to youngsters.

The 1980s were the Heather Duncan era. A heavy-set, muscular woman, Duncan was an on-again, off-again alcoholic whose thundering bellicosity was the bane of police and ambulance workers, who not infrequently attended her. Heather Duncan's temper often landed her in a mainland women's jail, which she considered a second home. In fact, one of her prized possessions was a jean jacket with the name of the jail spelled on the back in sequins. When not doing time, Heather Duncan sometimes lived in a Goodwill box. The first and only contact many Duncanites had with her was when a bag of used clothing they

Oliver Pipe.
Bert Kyle collection

Once renowned for its hunting and fishing, Duncan counts on Old Town character and totems to attract visitors. Top: CVM 980.1.2.8; bottom: 990.03.1.3a

had just crammed into the box came spitting back out with the comment, "Hey! This is my home."

In tone and substance, the City of Duncan's character has changed over the years, too. In the late 1800s and early 1900s, when farming was ascendant and the creamery anchored the city's economy, Duncan and the surrounding area were variously known as the Milk Bottle of Victoria, the Egg Basket of Canada, the Sweet Pea Capital of Canada. The Longstockings were recognized as the dominant force in the 1930s and Duncan was billed as the Most English Town in Canada. After World War II, the city unwittingly became known as Little Chicago (for its youth crime), Drunken Duncan (alcohol consumption), Little Detroit of the West (car lots) and "the ugliest little town on Vancouver Island." The last title was conferred by Donald Stainsby, a Vancouver journalist, who toured BC's small towns. In place of Duncan's once village-like air Stainsby found indistinguishable cinder block buildings, sidewalks stripped of trees,

plastic "Native" trinkets. Duncan looked like a spore of Burnaby, a clone of Port Coquitlam. "The quaint, doll-like city [is] today the most gaudy American town on Vancouver Island, if not the whole of British Columbia."

In 1985, then Duncan Mayor Douglas Barker decided to do something about Duncan's so-called image problem. Working with the Cowichan tribes, the City sponsored Native artists to carve totems and create a living museum in the town. Instead of existing side by side but independently, as the city and tribes had done for years, they began to interact and work together. The first poles in the project were carved in 1986. That year eleven totems were erected on the Trans-Canada

Lavern (Corky) Baines's "Rick Hansen Man in Motion" totem, 1999. Tom Henry photo

City of Totems, in a 1996 drawing by Ken Hicks.

Highway and two more around City Hall courtyard. The following years saw a steady addition of poles and carvings; by 1998 there were thirty-nine exhibits around the town. "I planted a seed," Barker later said. "Obviously it was a very fertile seed, because it has grown into a forest of totem poles."

The City of Totems, as Duncan billed itself, became a showcase mixture of traditional and free-form carving. A block west of Doug LaFortune's "Eagle Above Killer Whale With Spirit Helpers," inspired by traditional images and legends, rises a stylized creation entitled "La Fille des Dunes (Woman at the Beach)" by Quebec's Claude Tardif. "Cedar Man Holding Talking Stick" ("World's Largest in Diameter Totem"), by the celebrated carver Richard

Hunt, towers from what was the northwest corner of Chinatown. One of the most arresting pieces is Lavern Baines's "Rick Hansen Man in Motion" totem, prominently set in the cenotaph park at the corner of Trunk Road and Canada Avenue. Baines's pole depicts the Canadian wheelchair hero Rick Hansen atop a whale. Clutched in Hansen's hands is a globe and on the globe is an eagle. Glimpsed from the window of a vehicle hurtling along Trunk Road, the totem seems a disharmonious, gas-and-water concoction of ancient and modern. But observed from the shade of one of the park's red oaks, the bold form of the pole speaks clearly of the complex and still-evolving story playing out north of Strawberry Hill.

Appendix

City of Duncan Street Names

Alderlea Street: After William Duncan's farm, Alderlea. When Duncan had a townsite laid out on the west side of his property, he called it Alderlea (sometimes spelled Alder-lea). The name comes from the many alders that grew in the area.

Berkeley Street: From Rev. David H. Berkeley Holmes, who owned much of the property that became the Buena Vista subdivision.

Brae Road: From the Scottish *brae*, or hill. Kenneth Duncan's home, Brae Head, was at the north end of a track leading from his parents' home near Trunk Road. When a subdivision was laid out in the area in 1923, the track formally became Brae Road.

Bundock Avenue and **Whistler Street:** After William Whistler Bundock, who developed the surrounding subdivision.

Boundary Street: For the street that lay at what used to be the western limits of the city. Boundary extended from Government north to Cairnsmore Street. The Cairnsmore access was later replaced by Jubilee Street via Hospital Hill.

Brownsey Avenue: After William Brownsey, a developer.

Cairnsmore Street: After a location in Britain, where Reverend David Holmes was born. At one time all the property in the area was owned by Holmes's estate.

Campbell Road: After Jim Campbell, a developer.

Canada Avenue: Formerly Front Street; renamed by city council in 1927 to commemorate Canada's diamond jubilee of Confederation.

Cavell Street: Named in 1918 to commemorate the martyrdom of Nurse Edith Cavell, shot by German soldiers while aiding the escape of prisoners of war.

Charlotte Road (also **Powell Street**): After the Powell family, developers of the area.

Chesterfield Street: After Mayor James Chesterfield Wragg.

College Street: Named for its proximity to the schools.

Coronation Avenue: Originally named Relingferg Road, after a hamlet in Donegal, Ireland, birthplace of Mrs. Sarah Duncan; renamed in 1937 for the coronation of King George VI.

Craig Street: After John Craig, who assisted the surveyor E.B. McKay in laying out the business section of town, then settled in the area.

Day Road: After the Day family, subdividers.

Duncan Street: After the Duncan family, as it runs along what was formerly the Duncan preemption.

Evans Street: After James Evans, whose property adjoined the road.

Garden Street: Of uncertain origin. It was possibly named in honour of the live wire Vancouver mayor, Garden, or it was the place the Duncan family grew foodstuffs.

Government Street: Named for its location as the main road through Duncan to government offices.

Herbert Street: After Herbert Nadin Clague, who surveyed this property.

Holmes Street: After the David Holmes family.

Howard Avenue: After Howard Fry, a developer.

Ingram Street: After Sarah Annie Duncan, whose maiden name was Ingram.

Islay Street: After Islay Mutter, a businessman and politician (mayor, 1924–28). He was the son of a prominent Somenos farmer and sometime workmate of Robert Service.

Jubilee Street: Renamed in 1912 when the city was incorporated and three short streets were amalgamated: Jubilee Street, named for Queen Victoria's Jubilee when it was laid out; Lenora Street, between St. John's Church and St. John's Hall; and King's Road, to the bottom of Hospital Hill.

Kenneth Street: After Kenneth Duncan, son of William and Sarah Duncan and the city's first mayor.

Lomas Road: After William Henry Lomas, Indian Agent, who settled with his family on 40 hectares.

McKinstry Road, Watson Street and **Marchmont Road:** After Dr. McKinstry Watson, an early subdivider, whose family names include McKinstry and Marchmont. Before coming to Canada, Watson had interned on the estate of the Earl of Wharncliffe in Yorkshire. Those days were remembered in **York Road** (now part of the Trans-Canada Highway) and **Wharncliffe Road.**

Price Road: After the pioneer hotelier Frank Price, builder of the Quamichan and Tzouhalem Hotels.

Ypres, Festubert and **St. Julian Streets:** Formerly First, Second and Third Avenues; renamed for First World War battles in which Canadians figured prominently.

Selected Bibliography

Books and Papers

Barman, Jean. *The West Beyond the West: A History of British Columbia.* Toronto ON: University of Toronto Press, 1996.

Bowen, Lynne. *Those Lake People: Stories of Cowichan Lake.* Vancouver: Douglas & McIntyre, 1995.

Chan, Anthony B. *Gold Mountain: The Chinese in the New World.* Vancouver: New Star Books, 1983.

Connolly, Jay. *Duncan: City of Totems.* Duncan BC: City of Duncan, 1990.

Dunae, Patrick A. *Gentlemen Emigrants: From the British Public Schools to the Canadian Frontier.* Vancouver: Douglas & McIntyre, 1981.

Fisher, Robin. *Contact and Conflict: Indian-European Relations in British Columbia, 1774–1890.* Vancouver: UBC Press, 1992.

Forbes, Elizabeth. *Wild Roses at Their Feet: Pioneer Women of Vancouver Island.* Vancouver: British Columbia Centennial Committee, 1971.

Hayman, John. *Robert Brown and the Vancouver Island Exploring Expedition.* Vancouver: UBC Press, 1989.

Hutchison, Bruce. *The Unknown Country: Canada and Her People.* Toronto: Longmans, Green, 1942.

Ito, Roy. *We Went to War: The Story of the Japanese Canadians who served during the First and Second World Wars.* Stittsville ON: Canada's Wings Inc., 1984.

Jagpal, Sarjeet Singh. *Becoming Canadians: Pioneer Sikhs In Their Own Words.* Madeira Park BC: Harbour Publishing, 1994.

Lai, Chuen-yan David. *Chinatowns: Towns Within Cities in Canada.* Vancouver: UBC Press, 1988.

_____. *The Forbidden City Within Victoria: Myth, Symbol and Streetscape of Canada's Earliest Chinatown.* Victoria: Orca Book Publishers, 1991.

Lang, Catherine. *O-Bon in Chimunesu.* Vancouver: Arsenal Pulp Press, 1996.

Lillard, Charles. *Seven Shillings a Year: The History of Vancouver Island.* Ganges BC: Horsdal & Schubart, 1986.

Norcross, E. Blanche. *The Warm Land: A History of Cowichan.* Duncan BC: Island Books, 1975.

Olsen, W.H. *Water Over the Wheel: A Story of Mystery, Heartbreak and Success: the Chemainus Valley.* Chemainus BC: Schutz Industries, 1981.

Ormsby, Margaret A. *British Columbia: A History.* Toronto: Macmillan, 1958.

Pioneer Researchers, comp. *Memories Never Lost: Stories of the Pioneer Women of the Cowichan Valley and a Brief History of the Valley 1850–1920.* Duncan BC: Pioneer Researchers, 1986.

Queen Margaret's Historical Committee. *Beyond All Dreams: A History of Queen Margaret's School, Duncan, British Columbia.* Duncan BC: New Rapier Press, 1975.

Rozen, David. "The Ethnogeography of the Cowichan River, British Columbia." Unpublished paper, January 1977.

Service, Robert. *Ploughman of the Moon: An Adventure Into Memory.* New York: Dodd, Mead & Co., 1945.

Takata, Toyo. *Nikkei Legacy.* Toronto: NC Press, 1983.

Turner, Dolby Bevan. *When the Rains Came and Other Legends of the Salish People.* Victoria: Orca Book Publishers, 1992.

Weston, Jim and Stirling, David, eds. *The Naturalist's Guide to the Victoria Region.* Victoria: Victoria Natural History Society, 1986.

Williams, David R. *One Hundred Years at St. Peter's, Quamichan.* Duncan BC: Cowichan Leader, 1966.

Yorath, C.J. and Nasmith, H.W. *The Geology of Southern Vancouver Island: A Field Guide.* Victoria: Orca Book Publishers, 1995.

Zuehlke, Mark. *Scoundrels, Dreamers & Second Sons: British Remittance Men in the Canadian West.* N. Vancouver: Whitecap Books, 1994.

Periodicals

BC Historical News

Chinatown News

Cowichan Leader

Cowichan News Leader

The Citizen

Daily Colonist

Province

Seattle Times

Vancouver Sun

Victoria Times

Western Living

Maclean's

Acknowledgements

Many people contributed to *Small City in a Big Valley*. I am indebted to Duncan History Book Society members Lois Fenna, Ernie Moon, Ken McEwan, Myrtle Haslam and Priscilla Davis for overseeing the project. The latter two warrant special mention for their efforts. Haslam is an organizer par excellence and tirelessly advanced the book. Davis runs the superb Cowichan Valley Museum and was always kind when dealing with my many interruptions and requests. All members of the committee let me write the history of Duncan as I saw fit, even though they did not always agree with my approach. They also made many valuable suggestions. Responsibilty for errors of fact, or for any interpretation of Duncan's past, are mine alone.

Funding for the book was supported by businesses and families of the Duncan area and the City of Duncan. The British Columbia Heritage Trust also provided financial support.

The book also benefitted from the work of several writers: Jack Fleetwood, whose articles in the *Cowichan Leader* provide a useful chronology of Duncan history; journalist G.E. Mortimore's *Daily Colonist* profiles of Duncan citizens in the 1950s; and Tom W. Paterson's fine column, Chronicles. Elizabeth Blanche Norcross's *The Warm Land* and the Pioneer Researchers' *Memories Never Lost: Stories of the Pioneer Women of the Cowichan Valley and a Brief History of the Valley 1850–1920* were useful for the early history of the Cowichan Valley. Other contributors (of interviews, written submissions and research assistance) include Jack Davie, David R. Williams, Julie Roome, Jim Whittome, Margaret Rurrel, Gordon Purver, Bert Kyle, Keith Price, Charlie Clark, Tommy Clark, Marshal Haslam, Edna Macdonald, Patricia Lines, Jo Lennox, Shirley Garriock, Al Soderquist, historian Ian MacInnes, Norm and Phyllis Bomford, Bill and Joy Henry, Gwen Owens Smith, Jenny Lloyd, City of Duncan administrator Paul Douville, Paula Dickie, Kay Fujiwara (nee Toyota), Robert Cato, Queen Margaret's School director of development Mandy Parker and Cowichan Valley Museum assistant curator Tony Secord and summer student Ramon Bhullar. Information supplied to the Cowichan Valley Museum by Bob Evans, Jack Green, Gerald Prevost and Victor Jaynes was also valuable.

The section on Native history is based on information supplied by Abner

Thorne and Dianne Hinkley, articles by land claims researcher Linda Vanden Berg, and David Rozen's 1977 study "The Ethnogeography of the Cowichan River." Elders Arvid Charlie and Philomena Pagaduan assisted with translations.

The Chinatown chapter is largely based on the archival collection of the descendants of Suey Sing Chow.

Small City in a Big Valley benefitted from the editorial advice of Lorna Jackson.

Index